The Inner Teachings of Taoism

The Inner Teachings
of Taoism

by
Chang Po-tuan
Commentary by Liu I-ming

Translated by Thomas Cleary

Shambhala
Boston & London
2001

Shambhala Publications, Inc.
Horticultural Hall
300 Massachusetts Avenue
Boston, Massachusetts 02115
www.shambhala.com

Printed in the United States of America
This edition is printed on acid-free paper that
meets the American National Standards Institute
Z39.48 Standard. Distributed in the United States
by Random House, Inc., and in Canada by
Random House of Canada Ltd

The Library of Congress catalogues
the previous edition of this book as follows:
Liu, I-ming, 18th cent.
The inner teachings of Taoism.
Translation of: Chin tan ssu pai tzu chieh.
1. Chang, Po-tuan, 10th/11th cent. Chin tan ssu pai tzu
2. Taoism. 3. Alchemy—China—Early works to 1800.
I. Chang, Po-tuan, 10th/11th cent.
II. Cleary, Thomas F., 1949–
BL1900.C3563L5813   1986   299'.514   86-11841
ISBN 0-87773-363-5 (pbk.)
ISBN 1-57062-710-X (pbk.)

BVG 01

Contents

Introduction   vii

Part One
  The Inner Teachings   3
    EXPLANATORY VERSES   32
    TWENTY-FOUR ESSENTIALS FOR STUDENTS   36
    TWENTY-FOUR SECRETS OF ALCHEMY   40
    GLOSSARY   47

Part Two
  Solving Symbolic Language   51
    ON SYMBOLIC LANGUAGE   51
    ON GOING ALONG AND REVERSAL   54
    ON THE MEDICINES   56
    ON THE FIRING PROCESS   58

Part Three
  Related Texts   107
    FIFTY VERSES TO RESOLVE DOUBTS   107
    ON THE TRUE OPENING OF THE MYSTERIOUS FEMALE   116
    ESSENTIAL TEACHINGS FOR CULTIVATING REALITY   117

Introduction

Taoism is an ancient body of knowledge that has manifested itself in a multitude of diverse phenomena throughout Chinese history. So pervasive has the influence of Taoism been that it is difficult to name a single facet of Chinese civilization that has not been touched by it in some way. Politics, religion, science, medicine, psychology, art, music, literature, drama, dance, design, even warfare—in all these realms of endeavor are to be found phenomena bearing the characteristic stamp of Taoism.

There is an enormous body of specialist Taoist literature extant, containing a wide variety of technical lore. Much of this lore is couched in a number of esoteric languages, using such diverse formats as cosmology, mythology, religion, history, fiction, humor, magic, and alchemy. Needless to say, the problems of decoding this literature are formidable, for not only are there numerous codes, but even a single code may also be subject to a number of different interpretations.

The methods that have been employed in Taoist practice over the ages are also many and varied. Included in this vast range of techniques are physical, psychosomatic, and mental exercises, including special modes of movement, breathing, sexual intercourse, gazing, imagination and visualization, and dreaming. There are also many concentration exercises using such aids as special patterns of walking, thinking, and writing. Other exercises involve human service and the cultivation of certain types of social relations.

The Inner Teachings of Taoism

The earliest known Taoist text seems to be the *I ching*, well known as one of the fundamental Chinese classics, esteemed by both Confucians and Taoists. Composed in a time when divination was considered an integral part of the process of government, the core *I ching* writings have the outward form of oracles. Taoists consider the *I ching* one of the most detailed guides to human development, and the esoteric language of Taoist spiritual alchemy, a major teaching format, is largely based on the symbolism of the *I ching*.

After the *I ching*, the most famous and popular of Taoist classics is undoubtedly the *Tao te ching*. This text was compiled and recorded in a time of the decay of an ancient social order, a time when all writing considered serious dealt with sociopolitical issues. Not surprisingly, therefore, much of the *Tao te ching* is presented in terms of advice to rulers. Taoists consider this a fundamental text, drawing from it models of basic meditation techniques and mental postures. A large body of commentary and derivative literature is based on the *Tao te ching*, including other writings and lore associated with Lao-tzu, the reputed transmitter of this early classic.

Another extremely popular Taoist classic, the *Chuang-tzu*, was also written in this time of political deterioration, which was characterized by growing militarism and the predominance of sheer force over social contract. The *Chuang-tzu* has an air of humorous abandon, anarchy, satire, and unleashed imagination, envisioning an entirely new consciousness beyond the scope of then-current conceptions. Perhaps the first work of fantasy in Chinese literature that did not profess to be dynastic history, the classic *Chuang-tzu*, a dramatic release of the spirit, is widely considered one of the greatest literary masterpieces of all time.

Another classic apparently composed or compiled around this same time was the *Sun-tzu*, a famous treatise on military strategy. Although it is not usually referred to as a Taoist text per se, the *Sun-tzu* is nevertheless widely recognized as largely Taoist-inspired. While basically pacifistic, Taoism is not sentimental and has always recognized the reality of war. Rather than simply make moralistic pronouncements against war, Taoism approaches this problem realistically, using two basic strategies. The first of these is preventive, minimizing the causes of war existing in the human psyche; the second is palliative, minimizing the trauma of war when it actually does take place. The *Sun-tzu* shows what is now referred to as guerrilla warfare as a Taoistic type of strategy based on this idea of minimization of the actual violence and overall stress of warfare.

With the founding of the Han dynasty in the late third century B.C.E., the centuries of strife from which emerged such great Taoist classics as the *Tao te ching, Chuang-tzu,* and *Sun-tzu* came to an end. Taoistic laissez-faire government, characteristic of several Han dynasty reigns, allowed the economy to recover from generations of warfare and oppression; a great deal of interest was taken in natural science, with marked developments in agriculture and technology. There was also extensive intercourse between Taoism and Confucianism, resulting in the incorporation of certain Taoistic elements into the Confucian outlook.

One of the major Taoist texts dating from the Han period is the *Huai-nan-tzu,* composed by a group of Taoists at one of the minor courts. The *Huai-nan-tzu* recasts a great deal of ancient lore in a form suitable for its time, presenting the natural, human, and supernatural realms as a continuum in which the affairs of each realm reflect and are reflected by those of the others.

This vision of interreflection enabled Taoists to integrate secular and transcendental concerns harmoniously, and the *Huai-nan-tzu* includes discussions of political and military strategy as well as higher human evolution. The correspondence of the microcosm and the macrocosm, a characteristic theme, is also employed in a subtle way in the *Huai-nan-tzu,* inner psychic processes being represented metaphorically by such outer natural processes as the progress of the seasons. This device in particular became very popular later in the literature of Taoist spiritual alchemy.

Another product of the Han dynasty, destined to become one of the most important Taoist texts, is the cryptic *Ts'an t'ung ch'i,* or *Triplex Unity,* by the adept Wei Po-yang. This manual of spiritual alchemy became a major sourcebook for practitioners of the Complete Reality School of Taoism, which arose approximately one thousand years after the composition of the *Triplex Unity.* This difficult but intriguing book is still referred to in modern Taoist literature as the ancestor of alchemical treatises and is held in highest esteem.

Toward the end of the Han dynasty, growing political corruption and repression fostered spreading alienation among the intelligentsia as well as the peasantry. One characteristic manifestation of Taoism that arose from these conditions was the formation of intellectual circles of "pure conversation" involved in the study of human character and the creation of a new libertarian literature. On the other end of the social spectrum was popular Taoist freemasonry, which produced vigorous movement in society by grassroots organization and violent uprising.

After the fall of the Han dynasty, China was politically fragmented, with much of the north and west eventually being taken under the rule of alien dynasties. The breakdown of the political and intellectual monolith of the Han provided leeway for the entry of new elements into Chinese culture from southern and central Asia. One of the most powerful forces to enter China at this time was Buddhism, which figured prominently in the eventual rebirth of Chinese civilization after the turmoil of the post-Han generations.

Over the centuries following the dissolution of the Han dynasty, Buddhist texts were translated into the Chinese language at a prodigious rate, and Buddhist monastic orders were established on Chinese soil. At the same time, a parallel development took place in Taoism; large numbers of Taoist scriptures resembling those of the Buddhists were composed, and cloisters of Taoist monks and nuns were eventually set up on the Buddhist model.

Introduction

These Taoist scriptures were even classified after the manner of the Buddhist canon, and are often considered mere imitations of Buddhist scriptures, much like the Buddhicized Bon and Shinto writings of Tibet and Japan. The Taoist scriptures contain, however, certain elements whose parallels in Buddhism are to be found only in the esoteric forms of Tantric Buddhism, which never seem to have become very popular in China, in contrast to Tibet and Japan.

In addition to the great post-Han outflow of Taoist literature in religious garb, during this period there appeared two very famous classics employing older formats—the *Pao-p'u-tzu* and the *Lieh-tzu*. Both of these books go to great lengths to establish the idea that conventional knowledge is not ultimate, thus to expand the horizons of the human outlook; they approach the issue, however, from quite different angles.

The *Pao-p'u-tzu* places much emphasis on immortality and stresses the impossibility of assessing the question of the existence of immortals by ordinary standards based on common experience. The text contains a collection of alchemical recipes for elixirs that are supposed to transform human beings into immortals and transform base metals into gold.

It is by no means clear whether these recipes, obtained by the author of the *Pao-p'u-tzu* through extensive travel and research, were originally intended to be understood literally or metaphorically. There is ample evidence, however, that the supposed alchemical enterprise did involve considerable work and experimentation in chemistry and metallurgy as well as psychological development. The coexistence of material and spiritual alchemy was also paralleled in the West, and many outstanding personalities, such as Albertus Magnus, Ramon Lull, and Paracelsus, are associated with alchemy in Europe.

The author of the *Pao-p'u-tzu* was also a distinguished Confucian scholar who wrote many essays on social and political subjects.

These writings are collected in the so-called outer chapters of the *Pao-p'u-tzu,* forming a large proportion of the book. The same scholar also collected and transmitted legends of immortals, who were believed to intervene in human affairs from time to time and whose existence has been the subject of lively interest in China since remote antiquity.

The contents of the *Lieh-tzu,* in contrast, range from cosmology and metaphysics to satire. Among the ideas emphasized in this text are the interrelation of all phenomena and the limited nature of mental constructs used by the intellect to describe reality. A number of stories in the *Lieh-tzu* are drawn from the earlier *Chuang-tzu,* which it greatly resembles in certain ways. Some of these tales passed into popular lore and appear even in modern political and educational writings.

By the end of the sixth century C.E., China had been reunified, under the short-lived Sui dynasty. Public Taoist institutions were now well established, drawing many Buddhist monks and nuns into their ranks. A degree of friction developed between Taoism and Buddhism on the institutional level and continued for the next two or three centuries, with the salutary effect of allowing neither to become too complacent for too long.

The Sui dynasty was soon replaced by the T'ang dynasty (618–906), under which Chinese civilization enjoyed a new golden age, extending its cultural and economic influence into the surrounding nations of Asia. During the T'ang dynasty, Buddhism flourished, with a number of great specialist schools emerging into prominence. Nevertheless, Taoism still enjoyed considerable official favor and support; for a time civil service examinations based on Taoist classics were even established alongside the traditional conventional examinations in Confucianism.

A curious episode in the history of T'ang dynasty Taoism is the death of two emperors after ingesting alchemical immortality potions. The *Pao-p'u-tzu* notwithstanding, material alchemy and the

Introduction

search for literal physical immortality had in fact been repudiated centuries before in such classics as the *Chuang-tzu* and *Ts'an t'ung ch'i;* but repeated denunciation of such practices in later literature suggests that they continued to exist.

The incongruity of the age-old search for alchemical gold and physical immortality with the widely recognized evidence ancient Taoists give of advanced knowledge of psychological and physical realities only recently rediscovered by modern science has often led to the question of whether there was any real connection between different forms of activity lumped together under the name of Taoism. Although Taoist literature openly acknowledges the existence of ignorant experimentation and fraudulent practices, nevertheless it has been suggested that imperial poisonings were not mere superstitious bungling but intentional assassination; and that behind alchemical experimentation associated with Taoism was a conscious ploy to harness human greed to human progress by using it to motivate research in the natural sciences.

After the fall of the T'ang dynasty, various sects of Taoism continued to thrive, with increasing organization of sacred texts, rites, and local settlements. A Taoist canon was compiled in 1013, and an encyclopedic digest of its contents was also composed by the editors of the canon.

Not long after this collection of Taoist scriptures into a canon, three new schools arose, giving a new face to Taoism. These were the Absolute One, the True Great Way, and the Complete Reality schools. Active in northern China under alien rule, these attracted many followers from all walks of life. Many Buddhist centers, abandoned by Chinese Buddhists in the years of turmoil brought by the northern conquerors, were now taken over by these new Taoists.

The Complete Reality School, a highly purified form of Taoism showing a strong affinity with Ch'an (Zen) Buddhism, was particularly powerful and prominent, noted for its humanitarian works as well as its production of mystics of high attainment. During the Yuan dynasty (1279–1368), Complete Reality Taoists were charged with a new compilation of the Taoist canon, and thus the present form of the canon contains many works by adepts of this school.

Two main formats were employed by Complete Reality teachers and writers: records of sayings or short essays similar to those of the Ch'an Buddhist masters, and the ancient language of spiritual alchemy, largely based on the imagery of the *I ching*. Unlike Ch'an Buddhist works, however, the Complete Reality Taoist records of sayings, essays, and poetry include those of numerous female adepts; and unlike ancient alchemical texts, Complete Reality alchemical writings contain a considerable measure of explicit language.

One of the most important figures in the emergence of the Complete Reality movement was the eleventh-century adept Chang Po-tuan, who became known as the founder of the southern sect of the Complete Reality school. Chang is particularly known for his classic *Understanding Reality,* which has been a standard text of spiritual alchemy ever since, ranked on a par with the ancient *Triplex Unity.*

Born into a family of Confucian scholars, Chang Po-tuan continued in this tradition but eventually extended his interests into many fields, including astronomy, mathematics, and medicine. As his *Understanding Reality* attests, he also studied Ch'an Buddhism in depth and did extensive research in alchemical literature. According to his own statement, Chang was prompted to compose his alchemical treatises by the enormous confusion he found in the exegetical literature based on earlier alchemical works.

Although Chang spent many years associating with Buddhists and Taoists in search of transcendental knowledge, he was not to meet his real teacher until he was over eighty years of age. He then learned the Taoist secrets of restoration of vitality and energy, and ultimately mastered the spiritual teachings. He reached a high degree of mystic attainment and finally passed away at the age of ninety-nine after transmitting the inner teachings of Taoism through his writings and personal contacts.

Although Chang had a number of successful disciples, he is said to have been "punished by heaven" three times for passing on secrets of alchemy to unworthy people. After this he retired from the world and wrote his magnum opus, *Understanding Reality,* through which he said sincere people could learn the process of spiritual transformation.

Another of Chang's important writings, translated here as *The Inner Teachings of Taoism,* presents a summary of Taoist practice in the alchemical format. It is a simplified, condensed version of the teachings of *Understanding Reality,* giving the main outlines of the alchemical work in twenty short verses. This text is presented here with a modern explanation written by the great Taoist commentator Liu I-ming in 1808.

The Inner Teachings of Taoism became a very popular text, perhaps because of its brevity and accessibility. It was originally untitled, but later became known as *Four Hundred Words on the Gold Elixir.* According to Liu I-ming's introduction,

> The text is phrased in a simple and concise manner; the meaning is evident and clear. This work and Chang's *Understanding Reality* are like inside and outside: *Understanding Reality* gives a detailed breakdown of the "medicinal ingredients" and "firing process" of spiritual alchemy, whereas this treatise gives a general summary of the whole subject. The two works are one yet two, two yet one.
>
> Although this treatise has been annotated and explained many times since its composition in the Sung dynasty, these interpretations are either in terms of material alchemy or in terms of psychosomatic exercises: it is impossible to find a single commentary that conveys the reality, expresses the spirit, and reveals the hidden dimensions of this treatise.

I could not bear to let this precious work of the Founder be buried away, so I have made a detailed explanation of it, section by section, analyzing the metaphors and clearly pointing out what the "crucible," "furnace," "medicines," "firing," "doing," and "nondoing" are. Every word is clarified, every phrase analyzed; I have torn away the shell to expose the pit, broken open the bones to reveal the marrow. The jewels of this treasure chest are set out clearly in the open, in hopes that readers will understand at a glance and not be deceived by misleading interpretations.

Following his verse-by-verse elucidation of Chang Po-tuan's text, Liu I-ming gives a summary in classic fashion with twenty verses of his own composition. Because of the general nature of Chang's text, Liu then adds notes on essentials of Taoist study and secrets of alchemy, to clarify practical procedure in an orderly fashion. He explains this appendix in his introduction:

After finishing the explanation of Chang's text, I was still concerned that students might try to seek results without due regard for process, mistakenly hoping for immediate effects. Therefore I have added twenty-four essentials and twenty-four secrets, to enable students to proceed in an orderly fashion, ascending from lowliness to the heights. Those who practice with their feet on solid ground will eventually reach profound attainment of self-realization without wasting any effort.

Liu I-ming was one of the foremost interpreters of Taoist classics in his time, and from a modern point of view his commentaries are unsurpassed in clarity. Deeply versed in both noumenal Confucianism and Ch'an Buddhism, he was dedicated to restoring the original principles and practices of Complete Reality Taoism. He believed that a point had been reached where there was more harm than benefit in the practice of veiling the Taoist teachings in esoteric language, and undertook to reveal the meaning of the al-

chemical classics in plain language. To this end, he not only eluci-
dated the inner teachings of numerous ancient texts, but also
composed a systematic study of important terminology; as he
himself explains,

> Transmission of the true Tao has been lost for a long time, not
> just recently. After I had met genuine teachers, I compared
> the various alchemical classics and really found out the mean-
> ing of their symbolic language. Therefore I revealed what I
> had learned from my teachers in my explanations of the
> *Triplex Unity, Understanding Reality,* and other texts. Yet I still
> feared that students might have difficulty in gaining consis-
> tent and comprehensive understanding, so I wrote a treatise
> on symbolic language.

This exposition of Taoist symbolism is also presented in this volume, again with Liu's own poems summarizing each point under
discussion.

Generally speaking, Liu's explanations consist of three distinct
levels of presentation, and the key to reading his works in such a
way as to extract the essence of Taoist teaching lies in distinguish-
ing these three levels. The three types of presentation Liu uses may
be described as illustration of traditional use of esoteric terminology in Complete Reality teaching, repudiation of interpretations considered spurious by Complete Reality Taoists, and revelation of inner meaning in plain language.

In the course of his explanations, Liu will often speak in symbols, thereby demonstrating didactic manipulation of the esoteric
terminology of elements, yin and yang, *I ching* signs, and so on.
Since ancient times this manner of expression has been used for
several purposes: concealment, diversion, concentration, identifi-
cation of initiates and imitators, and stimulation of thought.

The use of symbolism is therefore an expedient, as the ancient
Tao te ching indicates, and its use depends on attendant circumstances. Liu's main purpose is to render esoteric language unneces-

sary, and the meaning of the teaching can be grasped without reference to these symbolic discourses. The value of Liu's symbolic presentations comes after the inner meaning is understood, as they can then be used as keys for unlocking the meanings of other alchemical texts.

Another secondary level of Liu's presentations is his repudiation of certain interpretations traditionally considered spurious by Complete Reality Taoists. These interpretations, and the practices based thereon, are generally referred to as "side doors" and are said to range from thoroughly aberrated and harmful "deviant paths" to useful but minor "auxiliary techniques" that may nevertheless sidetrack and injure untutored or obsessive enthusiasts. Liu explains:

> People of later times did not search out the meaning of the alchemical classics, but just stuck to the symbols: Confucians took them to be superstitious nonsense, while Taoists took them in a superficial manner. In extreme cases, people fixated on the symbols and arbitrarily invented all sorts of practices, getting caught up in sidetracks and deviant practices. Countless people have harmed themselves mentally and physically in this way. Surely this was not the intent of the ancients when they evoked images in symbolic language.

Repudiation of the "side doors" actually goes back at least as far as the *Chuang-tzu* and is even more explicit in the *Triplex Unity*, a millennium before the emergence of the Complete Reality School of Taoism. It is reiterated in many Complete Reality texts, but there are variations in the degree to which auxiliary techniques are accepted and applied by various teachers at various times.

In the southern sect of Complete Reality, founded by Chang Po-tuan, there is more emphasis on energy work than in the more austere northern sect, which Liu I-ming followed. This difference is explained by the advanced age of many initiates of the southern sect, beginning with Chang Po-tuan himself, who did not attain the Tao until he was in his eighties. Energy work, used for rejuvenation in order to sustain the spiritual work, is naturally often emphasized more, and in different forms, for older people than for younger people. In any case, these practices are said to be the most dangerous, and the need for expert guidance means that they may be publicly repudiated by those who practice them privately.

The critical aspect of Liu I-ming's work, rejecting the "side doors," may be viewed as representing the most radical form of the traditional Complete Reality distinction between the quintessence of Taoism and tangential physical or psychosomatic techniques. Two basic forms of the interpretations repudiated as spurious are false analogy and literal interpretation of symbolic expressions. While Liu also stressed the importance of vital energy and physical health, in interpreting Taoist symbolism he always rejected physical interpretations in favor of metaphysical interpretations.

The real marrow of Liu's texts, the main point of focus, generally follows symbolic discourses and precedes critiques of aberrations; this is when Liu shifts into plain language and provides an open explanation of the inner meaning of the passage under consideration. Sometimes these explanations are extremely brief, no more than a couple of sentences, but they provide the key to the whole book and present the points to look for in reading—what is known in Chinese as the "eye" of the work.

This small volume, when approached with these distinctions in mind, will yield an overall understanding of Taoism as it is presented in the alchemical format, in terms of three levels of realization: the reality, the appearance, and the illusion; or, in other words, the inner teachings, the outer husk, and the random spinoffs. In this sense, this volume is presented as an introductory study of a major manifestation of Taoism, including its principles, practices, and problems.

Part One

The Inner Teachings

1

Earth dwells in the center, as the mother of myriad beings. It is possible thereby to blend the elementary forces, produce and nurture myriad beings. Earth is that whereby origin and completion are effected. The true earth referred to here is not material earth; it is the true intent of the human body, which has no location. True intent is the director of myriad affairs; it controls the vital spirit, sustains essence and life, occupies and guards the center of the being. Because it has functions similar to earth, it is called true earth. Insofar as it is truthful and whole, without fragmentation, it is also called true faith. Because it contains the impulse of life within it, it is also called the center. Because it encloses everything, it is also called the yellow court. Because it is one in action and repose, it is also called the medicinal spoon. Because it can harmonize yin and yang, it is also called the yellow woman. Because it holds the pattern of the noumenon, it is also called the crossroads. There are many different names, all describing one thing, this true intent.

Lead is dense and heavy, hard and strong, lasts long without disintegrating; what is called true lead here is not ordinary material lead, but is the formless, immaterial true sense of real knowledge in the human body. This true sense is outwardly dark but inwardly bright, strong and unbending, able to ward off external afflictions, able to stop internal aberrations. It is symbolized by lead and so is called the true lead. Because its strength and vigor are within, it is also called the black tiger; because its energy is associated with metal, it is also called the white tiger. Because it is not constrained by things, it is also called iron man. Because its light illumines myriad existents, it is also called the golden flower. Because it is the pivot of creation, it is also called the North Star. Because it conceals light within darkness, it is also called metal within water. Because it contains masculinity within femininity, it is also called the rabbit in the moon. There are many different names, all describing this one thing, true sense.

Mercury is something lively and active, light and buoyant, soft and yielding, easily running off. Here what is called true mercury is not ordinary material mercury, but the formless, immaterial spiritual essence of conscious knowledge in the human body. The spiritual essence is outwardly firm yet inwardly flexible, utterly empty and metaphysical, unfathomable in its changing manifestations; call and it responds, touch it and it moves. It is symbolized by mercury, so it is called true mercury. Because it goes out and in unpredictably, it is also called the dragon. Because its energy is associated with the east, it is also called the blue dragon. Because it is developed by passing through tempering by fire, it is also called the red dragon. Because its nature is soft and loving, it is also called the wood mother. Because it is yang outside and yin inside, it is also called the girl. Because it contains femininity within masculinity, it is also called the raven in the sun. Because its reality is hidden within fire, it is also called mercury within cinnabar. Because its light is penetrating, it is also called flowing pearl. There are many different names used to depict this one thing, spiritual essence.

True intent, true sense, and spiritual essence are the three jewels in our bodies, true earth, true lead, and true mercury. These three jewels have a primordial, whole, unified energy, which is complete, without any defect. This cannot be called intent, sense, or essence—it is all one reality. But then when it mixes with temporally acquired conditioning, and yang culminates, giving rise to yin, the single energy divides into three. Thus there come to be the terms *intent, sense,* and *essence.* Once the real divides, the false comes forth; the seeds of routine take command, sense faculties and data stir together, and habit energy grows day by day: true intent becomes adulterated with artificial intentions, true sense becomes adulterated with arbitrary feelings, and spiritual essence becomes adulterated with temperament. Aberration and sanity mix, the artificial confuses the real, essence and life are shaken; day by day, year by year, the real disappears and all becomes false. Positivity exhausted, negativity complete, how can death be avoided?

When the real people have taught others to return to the fundamental and go back to the original, thereby to preserve essence and life, they have all taught people to restore these three things to reality. The path of restoration starts with knowing the original true intent. When you know the true intent, if you give your mind to it, the jewel of faith is in your hand; instantly all existents are empty, and you observe everything with detachment. External things cannot move you, and sane energy gradually arises. When consciousness of reality is constantly present, arbitrary feelings evaporate and true sense emerges, always responsive yet always calm, like true earth grabbing true lead so that the lead does not sink.

Once true sense appears, not concealing, not deceiving, the original spirit is always present and the discriminating spirit does not arise; then the temperament sublimates and the spiritual essence becomes manifest. This is like true lead controlling true mercury, so that mercury does not fly up.

The method of arresting and controlling is not a matter of

conscious contrivance; it is natural, spontaneous arresting and controlling, arresting without arresting, controlling without controlling. Because real truthfulness is in the center, the yin and yang of the sense of real knowledge and the essence of conscious knowledge cleave to one another, the two energies combine and congeal spontaneously.

What is difficult to accomplish in alchemy is the combination of essence and sense. The combination of essence and sense without imbalance is called centering. When the intent, essence, and sense meet, they are as before one energy; what had gone returns; what was lost is restored. This is like lead and mercury returning to the earth pot, stable and balanced, impervious to all conditioning influences. The illusory body and the stubborn mind naturally become quiet and still. The errant movements of the illusory body and the stubborn mind all come from separation of intent, essence, and sense; when these three are united, the real returns and the artificial quiesces—how could body and mind be stirred?

2

NOTHINGNESS PRODUCES WHITE SNOW;
QUIESCENCE PRODUCES YELLOW SPROUTS.
THE FIRE WARM IN THE JADE FURNACE,
OVER THE CRUCIBLE FLIES VIOLET MIST.

The previous section says that when mercury and lead return to true earth, body and mind do not stir; then one has entered the state of empty silence. But emptiness requires that emptiness reach the point where there is nothing to be emptied; only then is it called the ultimate of emptiness. Silence requires that silence reach the point of utter quiescence; only then is it called the ultimate of silence. When you reach nothingness, the primordial unity begins to emerge; when you attain quiescence, the primal true positive

[6]

energy comes back. Therefore the text says that "white snow" and "yellow sprouts" are produced. White snow symbolizes the energy of the primordial unity; this is like the metaphor of "white light arising in the empty room." "Yellow sprouts" appear with the return of the living potential; they symbolize the existence of movement within stillness. The empty room produces white light; when stillness culminates, there is movement; within black there is white; within yin there is yang—the primordial energy comes back, and the gold elixir takes form.

Once the gold elixir has form, it is urgent to use a gentle fire to incubate it, without either neglect or force, not slacking off for a moment. The "jade furnace" is the furnace of the flexibility of earth, symbolizing the calm serenity of the work, not being hasty or excited. The crucible is the crucible of the firmness of heaven, symbolizing firmness and stability of will, not changing. The "purple mist flying" symbolizes the sudden opening up of knowledge and wisdom when the work is consummated. When the spiritual sprouts are first born, use gentle fire to warmly nurture them, without either obsession or indifference, guarding against danger; progressing from weakness to strength, rawness to ripeness, when the firing is complete and the elixir is made, the light of wisdom shoots out—this is like violet mist flying up from the crucible when the medicine in the crucible is fully developed.

3

LOTUSES BLOOM IN THE FLOWER POND;
GOLDEN WAVES ARE QUIET ON THE SPIRITUAL WATER.
DEEP IN THE NIGHT, THE MOON JUST BRIGHT,
HEAVEN AND EARTH ARE IN ONE ROUND MIRROR.

The flower pond symbolizes the openness of consciousness; the spiritual water symbolizes true essence; the lotuses symbolize the light of wisdom; the golden waves symbolize objects of sense. When the spiritual sprouts have been warmly nurtured until their energy is complete, the flower of mind blooms and the light of wisdom arises. Therefore it says lotuses bloom in the flower pond. Once the light of wisdom arises, inwardly thoughts do not sprout, so essence is calm; then external things are not taken in and feelings are forgotten. Therefore the text says that the golden waves are quiet on the spiritual water. When essence is calm and feelings are forgotten, even if one is in the midst of myriad things, one is not deceived by myriad things. Round and bright, the mind is like the full moon shining deep in the night, its light pervading above and below, heaven and earth; the gold elixir crystallizes in the great void of space.

4

RED SAND REFINES TO POSITIVE ENERGY;
LIQUID SILVER COOKS INTO METAL VITALITY.
METAL VITALITY AND POSITIVE ENERGY,
RED SAND AND LIQUID SILVER.

The preceding three sections sum up the overall process of alchemy; from here on is a detailed analysis of the finer subtleties of the medicinal substances and firing process.

"Red sand" (cinnabar) is associated with the turbulence of the energy of fire and symbolizes volatility in people. "Liquid silver" (quicksilver) is associated with the movement natural to water and symbolizes the human mentality in people. Positive energy gives birth to beings; this symbolizes the real essence in people. The vitality of metal is luster; this symbolizes the consciousness of reality in people.

Lu Tsu said, "The seven-reversion restored elixir is a matter of people first refining themselves and awaiting the time." The classic

The Inner Teachings

Understanding Reality (*Wu chen p'ien*) says, "If you want to success-fully cultivate the nine-reversion, you must first refine yourself and master your mind." Shang Yang Tzu said, "Restoring the elixir is very easy; refining the self is very hard." These statements all say that if you want to practice the great Tao, you must first refine yourself.

The essential point in self-refinement starts with controlling anger and desire. The energy of anger is the aberrant fire of the volatile nature, which erupts upon confrontation and is indifferent to life, like a conflagration burning up a mountain, which nothing can stop. If you do not exert effort to quell it, refining it into something without smoke or flame, it can easily obscure reality. "Red sand refines to positive energy" means taking this volatility and refining it into neutral true essence.

As for desire, when the discriminating spirit of the human mentality sees objects and encounters things, it flies up; the senses become active all at once, and the feelings and emotions arise, like a gang of bandits stealing valuables, whom none can defend against. If you do not exert effort to block it and cook it into something that does not move or stir, it can easily thwart the process of the Tao. "Liquid silver cooks into metal vitality" means taking the human mentality and cooking it into the mindless consciousness of reality.

The extinction of the volatile nature and the appearance of true sense are like red sand transmuting into positive energy, ever to be warm, gentle essence. The death of the human mentality and the presence of consciousness of reality are like liquid silver changing into metal vitality, ever to be luminous mind.

Since reality is always there inside falsehood, and falsehood is not outside reality, when this nature and this mind go through the cooking and refining of fire, they become the real essence and the consciousness of reality. So the red sand turns to positive energy, and the liquid silver turns into metal vitality; if they are not put

[9]

through a refinement process, they will always be the volatile nature and the human mentality, and even positive energy will turn into red sand, even metal vitality will turn into liquid silver. Therefore the text says, "Metal vitality and positive energy, red sand and liquid silver." The false can become real, and the real can become false—the difference is a matter of refining or not refining. So practitioners should first quell anger and desire in order to refine the self. Restoring the elixir takes place momentarily; refining the self requires ten months. The work of refining the self is no small matter.

5

THE SOLAR YANG SOUL, THE FAT OF THE JADE RABBIT;
THE LUNAR YIN SOUL, THE MARROW OF THE GOLD RAVEN:
PUT THEM IN THE CRUCIBLE AND TRANSMUTE THEM
INTO A FLOOD OF WATER.

The preceding section speaks of the work of refining the self; this one speaks of the secret of gathering the medicines. The solar yang soul and the gold raven symbolize the finest part of conscious knowledge; the jade rabbit and the lunar yin soul symbolize the light of wisdom of real knowledge. Without the light of real knowledge, conscious knowledge cannot perceive far; without the manifestation of conscious knowledge, real knowledge cannot convey its light. Therefore the text says, "The solar yang soul, the fat of the jade rabbit; the lunar yin soul, the marrow of the gold raven," indicating that these two true medicines are to be put into the metaphysical crucible and quickly refined by fierce cooking with the true fire of concentration, causing them to mix and combine so that they merge like a flood of water, without the slightest pollution. Only then is the work done.

Conscious knowledge is flighty, and real knowledge easily becomes concealed: as soon as they act up, one should immediately put them back in the crucible and make them stay there, not letting them leave. This crucible is not a material crucible with form; as explained before, it is the crucible of firmness of heaven. This is the firm, strong, sane energy of the positive yang of heaven. When the sane energy is always present, unified awareness pure and true, the mind is stable and the will is far-reaching, growing stronger as time goes on, and real knowledge and conscious knowledge are forged into one whole.

6
THE MEDICINES ARE PRODUCED IN THE OCCULT OPENING; THE FIRING PROCESS ARISES IN THE YANG FURNACE. WHEN THE DRAGON AND TIGER HAVE MATED, THE GOLD CRUCIBLE PRODUCES A MYSTIC PEARL.

The medicines are the medicines of real knowledge and conscious knowledge. The occult opening is an opening of profound subtlety, where yin and yang divide, and also where essence and life abide. This is what is called the opening of the mysterious pass. This opening has many different names—the opening of the mysterious female, the door of birth and death, the house of enlivening and killing, the opening of nothingness, the gate of myriad wonders. All these terms refer to the same thing.

This opening is not existent, not nonexistent, not material, not void; it has no location or form, but is in ecstasy and profound abstraction. It is not inside or outside. If you try to find it in terms of place or form, you will miss it by a long shot.

The firing process is the process of the work. The yang furnace is the work of intensive refinement by fierce cooking. It is not that there really is a furnace; because of the use of firing work to refine the medicines of real and conscious knowledge, it is called a furnace.

The dragon is associated with wood and symbolizes essence,

emerging from conscious knowledge. The essence of conscious knowledge transforms unfathomably, so it is represented as a dragon. The tiger is associated with metal and symbolizes sense, emerging from real knowledge. The sense of real knowledge is firm and strong and unbending, so it is represented as a tiger.

There is temperamental nature, and there is innate essence; there is emotional feeling, and there is unerring sense. Temperamental nature is acquired, whereas innate essence is primal; emotional feeling is secondary, whereas unerring sense is inherent.

The gold crucible is the crucible of the firmness of heaven. The mystic pearl is another name for the gold elixir. Because the gold elixir pill is round and bright, it is represented as a pearl; because its spiritual subtlety is hard to express, it is also represented as a mystic pearl.

The preceding section said that the solar yang soul and the lunar yin soul transmute into one flood—the gold elixir is formed. But in alchemy the production of the medicines has its time and the operation of the fire has its process; if you do not know the time of the production of the medicines and the process of the operation of the fire, the gold elixir will not crystallize. In *Understanding Reality,* our author writes, "Even if you know the cinnabar and lead, it is useless if you do not know the firing process. It all depends on the power of practical application; the slightest deviation, and you will fail to crystallize the elixir."

When the two medicines, real knowledge and conscious knowledge, arise in the occult opening, one should take the opportunity to get to work, intensely refining them to burn away conditioned temperament and emotional feeling, overcome the ordinary dragon and ordinary tiger, and cause the true dragon and true tiger of primordial true essence and sense to mate in the gold crucible, becoming inseparably bound to one another, naturally producing a mystic pearl which is round and bright, pervading the universe without obstruction.

However, when these medicines arise in the occult opening, sharing the qualities of heaven and earth, sharing the light of sun and moon, sharing the order of the four seasons, they are difficult to obtain and easy to lose. When the firing process conforms to what is appropriate, the real solidifies while the false evaporates, and the gold elixir immediately crystallizes. If the firing process is even slightly off, the real departs while the false comes, and you stumble by even while it is right before you. The classic *Guide to Putting in the Medicine* (*Ju yao ching*) says, "Reception of energy is fortunate; prevent it from turning into disaster." It is necessary to be careful.

7

THIS OPENING IS NOT AN ORDINARY APERTURE:
MADE BY HEAVEN AND EARTH TOGETHER,
IT IS CALLED THE LAIR OF SPIRIT AND ENERGY;
WITHIN IT ARE THE VITALITIES OF WATER AND FIRE.

The preceding section said that the occult opening can produce the medicines. Because this opening is most abstruse and subtle, in ecstasy and deep abstraction, if you aim for it, you lose it; if you conceptualize it, that is not it. It is not one of the ordinary apertures in the body, which have form and shape and can be pointed to; it is formless, invisible, a sacred opening that cannot be pointed out. In the human body, this opening is not the "yellow court" (between the heart and navel), not the "crimson chamber" (at the solar plexus), not the "field of elixir" (below the navel), not the "ocean of energy" (below the navel), not the coccyx, not in front of the kidneys and behind the navel, not the space between the kidneys and the genitals, not the middle of the spine where the ribs join, not the active and passive energy channels, not the "luminous hall" (an inch behind the midpoint between the brows), not the "center of tranquillity" (in the midbrain), not the "celestial valley" (at the top of the head), not the "jade pillow" (at the back of the head), not the mouth and nose. Its creation has to do with the yin and yang energies of heaven and earth joining in the center of space.

HEAVEN ☰ is firm, associated with yang; EARTH ☷ is flexible, associated with yin: when the two energies, firm and flexible, join together, then there is this opening. When the two energies, firm and flexible, are separate, this opening does not exist. Metaphorically, the open space between heaven above and earth below is this occult opening.

If people have firmness without flexibility, or are only flexible and not firm, this is solitary yin or isolated yang—with the adulterated energy therein suffocatingly full, how can there be the occult opening? Since there is no occult opening, the dynamic of energy has ceased—how can it produce medicine? Therefore the text says the occult opening is made by HEAVEN and EARTH together.

Because it is made by combination of HEAVEN and EARTH, it is also called the lair of spirit and energy. Spirit is the subtlety of consciousness that is beyond conception; energy is the harmonious living potential. Spirit is yin within yang, represented as FIRE ☲ and as the sun. Energy is yang within yin, represented as WATER ☵ and as the moon.

Heaven and earth, yin and yang, join together, with an opening in the center space, wherein sun and moon come and go; when people's firmness and flexibility join together, there is an opening in the center space, wherein spirit and energy congeal. The principle is the same. Therefore it is called the lair of spiritual energy, with the vitalities of WATER and FIRE in it.

People are born endowed with the vitalities of sun and moon (yang and yin), so the spirit and energy in the body are the vitalities of WATER and FIRE.

This opening cannot be sought consciously, nor can it be grasped unconsciously. Though one depends on personal instruction from a teacher, still it must be realized by oneself. When you discover this opening, WATER and FIRE, the medicines, appear at hand and need not be sought externally. Right away you can cull them at will. It is too bad that students everywhere practice concentration on specific defined "apertures" in the head and torso—how can they stabilize spirit and energy and preserve essence and life that way?

8

WOOD MERCURY, ONE DASH OF RED;
METAL LEAD, THREE POUNDS OF BLACK.
MERCURY AND LEAD COMBINE INTO GRANULES
THAT SHINE VIOLET-GOLD.

The preceding section said that the occult opening has the vitalities of WATER and FIRE; it is by the vitalities of FIRE and WATER that the elixir can be formed. The vitality of fire is wood and mercury; wood and mercury are buoyant and symbolize spiritual essence. The vitality of water is metal lead; metal is dense and tends to sink, and symbolizes true sense. Spiritual essence, containing the fire of open awareness, is conscious knowledge, yang outside and yin inside. The yin is less than the yang; yin hides inside the yang. That inside yin is associated with fire, so it is called "one dash of red." True sense, containing stable sane energy, is real knowledge, yin outside and yang inside. The yang is less than the yin; yang hides inside the yin. That outside yin is associated with water, so it is called "three pounds of black."

"One dash of red" symbolizes a small amount; "three pounds of black" symbolizes a large amount—it is not that there really are measures of one dash and three pounds. The method of alchemy involves gathering the bit of true fire of open awareness within conscious knowledge and refining out the adulterating energy of confused feelings, then gathering the pure spiritual water of desirelessness within real knowledge and extinguishing the baseless burning of the temperament. When the true fire and spiritual water join into one, water and fire balance each other, true feeling and spiritual essence combine, and real knowledge and conscious knowledge cleave to one another; then sense is itself essence, and essence is itself sense. Utterly conscious of reality, consciousness utterly real, the unified energy functions the same as heaven and earth. This is likened to lead and mercury being forged into spiritual granules; when the firing is complete, the medicine is perfected and turns violet-gold, never again to change.

9

THE HOME GARDEN'S SCENERY IS BEAUTIFUL;
THE WEATHER IS THAT OF SPRING.
WITHOUT WORKING WITH PLOW AND HOE,
THE WHOLE EARTH IS GOLDEN.

The preceding section said that the elixir can be compounded with lead and mercury. People might suppose that this means it is made by forging ordinary material lead and mercury, but they still do not realize that these are not the ordinary material substances, but are the beautiful scenery of the home garden within oneself. Since real knowledge and conscious knowledge, which are one's own true lead and mercury, are naturally present in one's home, they need not be sought externally; the scenery is beautiful. Yin and yang being in harmony, the mechanism of life unceasing, is like the weather in spring; the medicinal sprouts grow, without needing the work of plow and hoe. White snow flies, filling the sky; everywhere there grow yellow sprouts, which you can gather as you go along—everything is the Tao; wherever you walk there is treasure at every step, as though the whole earth were gold.

10

TRUE LEAD ARISES IN WATER;
ITS FUNCTION IS IN THE PALACE OF FIRE:
TURNING BLACK TO RED,
FOG IS THICK IN THE CRUCIBLE.

The preceding section says the scenery is inherent in the home garden; nevertheless, though it is inherent, it is not at your command without thoroughgoing work. Because the lead of real knowledge is sunken into yin, it is symbolized by the WATER trigram ☵ , yin outside and yang inside, yang enclosed by yin, acquired influences covering up the inherent sane energy so that the sane energy cannot get out by itself. If you want to bring it out, the function is in the palace of FIRE ☲ ; conscious knowledge, solid outside and empty inside, is symbolized by the FIRE trigram, containing the true fire of open awareness. When you use this true fire to burn away acquired influences, then real knowledge appears and merges with conscious knowledge, turning black to red, real knowledge becoming conscious knowledge. Yang, capturing yin, obtains nurturance; yin and yang cleave to one another, producing a harmonious energy, like a thick fog staying inside the crucible without dispersing.

11

TRUE MERCURY COMES FROM FIRE;
ITS FUNCTION IS IN WATER.
THE MAIDEN GOES TO THE SOUTH GARDEN;
HER HAND GRIPS THE JADE BALUSTRADE.

The true mercury, conscious knowledge, secretes the adulterated energy of discriminatory awareness; it is symbolized by the trigram

FIRE ☲ , being light outside and dark inside. The discriminatory awareness uses consciousness to produce illusions; seeing fire, it flies—without the lead of real knowledge to control it, the discriminating awareness would cause trouble, and it would be impossible to return to reality. Therefore, the function lies in WATER. WATER symbolizes real knowledge, which has the pure "water" of true unity. When you use this pure water to extinguish the aberrant fire of discriminatory awareness, after the aberrant fire goes out, conscious knowledge returns to reality. The "south garden" represents FIRE; the "jade balustrade" represents WATER; the "maiden" is another name for conscious knowledge, so called because conscious knowledge is yin within yang. When conscious knowledge is controlled by real knowledge, yin comes to yang and is not moved by external things; conscious knowledge cleaves to real knowledge, real knowledge cleaves to conscious knowledge. This is "the maiden going to the south garden, her hand gripping the jade balustrade," the functions balancing and completing one another.

12

THUNDER AND LAKE ARE NOT EAST AND WEST;
WATER AND FIRE ARE NOT NORTH AND SOUTH.
THE HANDLE OF THE DIPPER CIRCLES THE HEAVENS,
REQUIRING PEOPLE TO UNDERSTAND HOW TO AGGREGATE.

The preceding sections speak of wood/mercury, metal/lead, water, and fire mixing together; people often imagine these terms to apply to forms and locations within the body, associating fire with the heart and the south, associating water with the genitals and the north, associating wood with THUNDER and the liver and the east, associating metal with LAKE and the lungs and the west. They just take the heart, genitals, liver, and lungs for WATER ☵ , FIRE

☲ , THUNDER ☳ , and LAKE ☱ , and have actually not gotten the true tradition. They still do not know that THUNDER stands for our true essence, LAKE stands for our true sense, WATER stands for our real knowledge, and FIRE stands for our conscious knowledge. These four are the primordial true "four forms" inherent in us; because of mixture with acquired adulterated energy, they each dwell in a separate place and cannot join. Now, if you want to restore them to unity as one energy, this requires the work of aggregation.

The work of aggregation means turning the celestial mechanism of the dipper handle. The dipper handle is the fifth, sixth, and seventh stars of the Big Dipper. Where these stars sit is unlucky; what they point to is lucky. They turn, as it were, the constellations through the heavens in the course of a year. In the human body, this refers to the point of true sense of real knowledge. One name of true sense is the iron man, in that it is strong and unbending, able to give life and to kill; this is also like the dipper handle in the sky. After birth, it is polluted by external influences, seduced by external things; the dipper handle points outward, not inward; the enlivening energy is outside, the killing energy is inside. Following the course of nature, the young mature, the mature age, the aged die; this goes on and on in repetitious cycles, with no hope of escape. If one knows the mechanism of life and death and turns around the dipper handle, when one changes one's orientation, one arrives at one's homeland and can thereby take over the evolutionary cycle and thus join the four forms and five elemental energies, so that the elixir soon forms, without effort.

But most people cannot recognize the dipper handle of true sense; they mistakenly take physical locations in the four directions in the body to be THUNDER, LAKE, WATER, and FIRE, and indulge in bogus practices, vainly imagining formation of the elixir. Does no one wonder why they struggle all their lives, only to grow old with no attainment? Is this not to be lamented?

13

THE FIRING PROCESS DOES NOT CALL FOR SET TIMES;
THE WINTER SOLSTICE IS NOT IN DECEMBER.
AS FOR THE RULES FOR BATHING, SPRING AND AUTUMN
ARE ALSO METAPHORS WITHOUT REALITY.

The preceding section states that THUNDER, LAKE, WATER, and FIRE have special meanings and are not east, west, south, north. Not only that; when it says in the alchemical classics to advance the yang fire in December, repel the yin convergence in May, and bathe in spring and autumn, these are all just metaphors, without literal reality. They do not really mean the four seasons.

In the course of nature's cycle, the time when yang energy first emerges from the earth is called the time of the rat, which corresponds to the month of December and the hour of midnight. The time when yin energy first emerges from the earth is called the time of the horse, which corresponds to the month of May and the hour of noon. The time when yang energy has risen midway between heaven and earth is called the time of the hare, which corresponds to the spring equinox and the hour of six A.M. The time when the yin energy has risen halfway between heaven and earth is called the time of the bird, which corresponds to the autumn equinox and the hour of six P.M. So the rat and the horse are the times when yin and yang have just arisen, and the hare and the bird are the times when yin and yang are level. These are the rat, horse, hare, and bird of the Tao of nature.

The Tao of alchemy takes the time of the rat as the time to advance the yang fire, because when a point of yang light appears in the body, it is like the winter solstice in December. When one yang subtly arises, one should quickly advance the fire and gather it, assisting this bit of faint yang to gradually grow and develop, not letting it fade away. This is what is called advancing the fire of yang in December, or at midnight, the time of the rat.

The time of the horse is taken to be the time for repelling the yin convergence because the arising in darkness of a point of yin energy in the body is like the summer solstice in May of the lunar calendar. When one yin comes to join, one should quickly work to repel it, suppressing this bit of false yin, evaporating it as it grows, not letting up for a moment. This is what is called operating the yin convergence.

In reality, yang and yin arise all the time. The arising of yang is the time of the rat; the arising of yin is the time of the horse. These are the living rat and horse within our bodies, not the dead rat and horse of the calendar and clock. Therefore it says that the process does not call for set times and the "winter solstice" is not in December. The reason it mentions the time of the rat (December/midnight) and not the time of the horse (May/noon) is that the horse is contained within the rat. An ancient immortal said, "No need to look for the rat and the horse in the season or time of day; within the body there is naturally one yang arising." Seeing this, we can know that the winter solstice is not in December.

The Tao of alchemy takes spring and autumn, or six A.M. and six P.M., as appropriate for bathing, because after the point of yang light in the body has returned, it gradually grows and harmonizes with yin energy, neither too much nor too little, returning to balance, and this is like the yang energy on earth in spring rising to midway between heaven and earth at the spring equinox; one should stop the firing and make the yin and yang equal and harmonious, not advancing the fire excessively—this is the reason for "bathing." It does not mean one should bathe at the spring equinox. And when the point of yin energy in the body comes to join, as it grows it recedes and joins with yang energy, without imbalance, entering the mean. It is also like the yin energy in autumn rising to midway between heaven and earth at the autumn equinox; one should stop working and balance the firmness and flexibility, not repelling the yin excessively—this is the reason for "bathing." It does not mean one should bathe at the autumn equinox. Therefore, the text says that in the rules for bathing, spring and autumn are also metaphors without reality.

Our author's *Understanding Reality* says, "When the moon in the east and west reaches its season, punishment and reward are at hand; medicine is patterned on this." So we know that when advance and recession in the growth of the medicine are spoken of in terms of spring and autumn, it does not mean literally that one should bathe in spring and autumn. Later people did not know the metaphorical language of the alchemical classics and supposed that they mean to advance yang in December and at midnight, the month and hour of the rat, and to repel yin in May and at noon, the month and hour of the horse, then to bathe at the spring equinox and six A.M. and at the autumn equinox and six P.M., the months and hours of the hare and bird. But if you use the calendar and clock to figure the rat, horse, hare, and bird, think of this: the terms *rat, horse, hare,* and *bird* are applied to years, months, days, and hours alike—which do you take for the rule? Isn't this a big mistake? When our author says that the winter equinox is not in December, and that spring and autumn are also empty metaphors, he gets rid of the misapprehensions of all those who have gone off on tangents, and tells students to make a careful distinction based on the real pattern. What can compare to that compassion?

14

THE RAVEN'S LIVER AND THE RABBIT'S MARROW—
GRAB THEM AND PUT THEM BACK IN ONE PLACE.
GRAIN AFTER GRAIN, FROM VAGUENESS TO CLARITY.

The preceding section says that the firing process and bathing are not in the times of the rat, horse, hare, and bird; it is all a matter of teaching people to know the harmonization of essence and sense, the same energy of yin and yang. "The raven's liver" is the vitality of the sun; liver is dark, which is associated with wood, and so symbolizes the essence of conscious knowledge. "The rabbit's marrow" is the light of the moon; marrow is white, which is associated with metal, so it symbolizes the sense of real knowledge. Conscious knowledge and real knowledge, true essence and true sense, are the great medicines used in cultivating the elixir. Taking these four and putting them together, operating the fire to cook and refine them, they transmute into one energy. One energy undifferentiated, the living potential is ever-present, unfailingly growing from one yang to gradually reach the pure wholeness of six yangs, going from vague to clear, the gold elixir developing naturally. Here, "grab" does not mean forced action or effort; it means causing them to remain and not letting them leave. When they stay put, mixed thoughts do not arise and external influences do not enter; the four are gathered in one place and do not conflict with one another. "Grain after grain" means that when the basis is established, the path develops and the yang energy gradually grows; it does not literally mean there is the form of grains.

15

THE UNDIFFERENTIATED CONTAINS SPACE;
SPACE CONTAINS THE WORLD:
WHEN YOU LOOK FOR THE ROOT SOURCE,
IT IS THE SIZE OF A GRAIN.

The preceding section said the elixir can be made by the raven's liver and the rabbit's marrow. This elixir is nothing but the energy of primordial true unity inherent in our original, undifferentiated beginning. This energy envelops space, and space envelops the world. Enveloping space and the world, its size is measureless; yet even though it is measureless, when you search out its root source, it is no bigger than a grain. And though it is said to be like a grain, yet it is imperceptible and ungraspable: "Vague and indefinable, therein is an image; indefinable and vague, therein is something. Dark and occult, therein is a vitality; that vitality is most real, therein is true experience." This image, this thing, this vitality, this experience, are all what is called the energy of primordial unity. This energy is the origin of heaven and earth, the mother of myriad things. It is truly empty yet contains ineffable existence, ineffably existing while inherently truly empty. It has nothing to do with great or small; it cannot be defined as being or nonbeing; it is neither material nor vacuous, yet both matter and emptiness. Let it go and it is everywhere; roll it up and it hides in mystery. Its concealment and revelation are unfathomable; its transmutations are unpredictable. How can any concrete object be compared to it? If you know the unitary energy within nondifferentiation, when you know the One, myriad tasks are done, and practicing the Tao is not difficult.

16

HEAVEN AND EARTH SHARE THE LIQUID OF REALITY;
SUN AND MOON CONTAIN THE VITALITY OF REALITY.
WHEN YOU UNDERSTAND THE FOUNDATION
OF WATER AND FIRE,
THE WORLD IS IN YOUR BODY.

The preceding section said that one grain can contain space and the world. But the reality of this grain is inherent in our body and need not be sought elsewhere. It is only necessary to understand how to harmonize yin and yang. When yin and yang are not in harmony, the energy of primordial unity does not return and the gold elixir does not crystallize.

Observe how when heaven and earth mate, the liquid of reality descends and fosters the growth of myriad beings and things; when sun and moon mate, the vitality of reality circulates and brings about the four seasons. This is when yin does not leave yang and yang does not leave yin; yin and yang join, containing the liquid of reality and the vitality of reality—only then is there creation. Otherwise, solitary yin does not give birth, solitary yang does not foster growth; the mechanism of life has ceased, so where can creation and evolution come from?

Our conscious knowledge and real knowledge are the heaven and earth and sun and moon in our bodies. Conscious knowledge has the yang energy of heaven, so it is heaven. The light emanated by the yang energy is like the hollow in the FIRE trigram ☲ , which hollow is the sun. Real knowledge has the yin energy of earth, so it is earth. The fine essence secreted by the yin energy is like the fullness in the WATER trigram ☵ , which fullness is the moon. So heaven and earth, sun and moon, are all inherent in our bodies. It is just that people do not know how to harmonize them, so yin and yang are separated and the enlivening potential fades away, ultimately returning to the Great Flux.

If you understand that the foundation of WATER and FIRE of real knowledge and conscious knowledge originally belong to one energy, and if you cultivate them backward, inverting WATER and FIRE, using real knowledge to control conscious knowledge, using conscious knowledge to nurture real knowledge, water and fire balance each other, movement and stillness are as one; then mind is Tao, Tao is mind, mind is the mind of Tao, body is the body of Tao, sharing the qualities of heaven and earth, sharing the light of sun and moon, sharing the order of the seasons—the whole world is within one's own body.

17

THE DRAGON COMES FROM THE EASTERN SEA;
THE TIGER COMES FROM THE WESTERN MOUNTAINS.
THE TWO BEASTS HAVE A BATTLE
AND TURN INTO THE MARROW OF HEAVEN AND EARTH.

The preceding section said that if you understand the foundation of WATER and FIRE, the great Tao can be attained. WATER and FIRE are symbols of real knowledge and conscious knowledge; if you want water and fire to balance and settle each other, it is necessary first to join metal and wood.

Essence is associated with wood; dwelling in the east, it is the property of the self, and because of its unfathomable fluidity it is likened to a dragon. Sense is associated with metal; dwelling in the west, it is the property of the other, and because of its unbending strength it is likened to a tiger.

However, essence and sense both have differences in terms of being true or false, primal or conditioned. The essence of round luminosity and the formless sense are the true primal; the temperament and feelings tied to objects are the false and conditioned. After we are born, the false mixes in with the true; the dragon becomes fierce, the tiger becomes wild, and they dwell apart, not communicating. Unless we get rid of the false and rescue the true, the great Tao is unattainable.

When the text says that "the dragon comes from the eastern sea," it means chasing the dragon to the tiger, using essence to seek sense. When it says that "the tiger comes from the western mountains," it means leading the tiger and riding the dragon, using sense to return to essence. When essence and sense meet, use sense to stabilize essence, use essence to control sense; when essence and sense are bound together, their fierceness and wildness become docility and harmony: the false vanishes and the true returns. Essence loves sense, obedient and dutiful; sense loves essence, kind and benevolent. When metal and wood, sense and essence, join together, this is the complete Original Face without defect. Therefore the text says that "the two beasts have a battle and turn into the marrow of heaven and earth."

The word *battle* has a deep meaning. Once people's primal yang culminates and mixes with temporal conditioning, the senses and their objects as they have been conditioned through history become active, and feelings and emotions run amok; add to this the acquired energies of habits accumulated in this life, and inside and outside are all yin, which cannot easily be stripped away. Without intense effort to strip away this conditioning acquired through cultural and personal history, how can it be extinguished? Properly speaking, *battle* means vigorous and intense refinement, which effort is not to be relaxed until yin is exhausted and yang is pure. "Turning into the marrow of heaven and earth" means pure unity without duality when essence and sense have been purged of all pollution; only then is the work done. The subtle meaning of this stage is expressed in our author's *Understanding Reality* in these lines: "The white tiger of the western mountains is very wild; the blue dragon of the eastern sea cannot stand up to it. Grabbing them with both hands, make them engage in mortal combat; they will change into a cluster of violet-gold frost."

Indeed, essence and sense are not easy to harmonize. It takes years of intense effort before it is possible to return to reality.

18
GOLD FLOWERS BLOOM WITH MERCURY PETALS;
JADE STEMS GROW ON LEAD TWIGS.
WATER AND FIRE HAVE NEVER BEEN SEPARATE;
HOW LONG DO HEAVEN AND EARTH ENDURE?

The preceding section is on the joining of metal and wood, the union of essence and sense; this section immediately follows upon that, expressing the effect of the joining of metal and wood.

"Gold flowers" and "lead twigs" are associated with yang, which is firm, and refer to true sense. "Mercury petals" and "jade stems" are associated with yin, which is flexible, and refer to true essence. The center of FIRE ☲ is open; openness is associated with yin, and is conscious knowledge. The center of WATER ☵ is full; fullness is associated with yang, and is real knowledge. "Gold flowers bloom with mercury petals" means there is flexibility within firmness, sense being none other than essence; "jade stems grow on lead twigs" means there is firmness within flexibility, essence being none other than sense. "WATER and FIRE have never been separate" means that fulfillment contains emptiness and emptiness contains fulfillment; real knowledge is conscious knowledge, and conscious knowledge is real knowledge.

Able to be firm, able to be flexible, able to be empty, able to be full, firmness and flexibility corresponding, emptiness and fulfillment including each other, tranquil and imperturbable yet sensitive and effective, sensitive and effective yet tranquil and imperturbable, going through the same processes as heaven and earth, thus one shares the eternity of heaven and earth—when will there ever be destruction?

19
BATHE AND WARD OFF DANGER,
EXTRACT AND ADD, TAKING CARE.
IN ALL, THERE ARE THIRTY THOUSAND INTERVALS;
BEWARE OF EVEN THE SLIGHTEST SLIP.

The preceding section speaks of the merging of essence and feeling, the congealing of real knowledge and conscious knowledge, whereupon the elixir forms. But though the medicinal substances are easy to know, the firing process is most difficult. If you do not know the details of operating the fire, and slip up even a little bit, it will cause a tremendous miss and the gold elixir cannot be formed.

After the elixir has been restored, there is a time for bathing and a process of extraction and addition. Before the medicines are obtained, one must refine the self to gather medicine; after the elixir is obtained, one must bathe to incubate it. Bathing means the work of warding off danger.

An ancient immortal said, "The elixir is restored in a short time; incubation requires ten months." In ten months there are thirty thousand intervals; during each interval one keeps attentive to ward off danger, like a hen sitting on an egg, like an oyster embracing a pearl, focusing single-mindedly on the sphere of attention. One also works on extracting lead and adding mercury, carefully guarding against any slip-up. If there is any slip-up, this produces falsehood within reality; external influences sneak in, and the gold elixir, once gained, is again lost, forms but then decays. Then the problem of burning the crucible cannot be avoided.

Therefore in alchemy the work of warding off danger is indispensable, start to finish. Warding off danger means preventing external influences from creeping in and taking care that the basis of the elixir is not damaged. When we speak of warding off danger, the work of extraction and addition is therein. Extraction means taking out the lead; addition means putting in the mercury. Before the elixir is crystallized, one must use true lead to control true mercury; once the mercury is inert and the elixir has crystallized, it is necessary to extract this lead energy again before the true mercury can become a spiritual jewel. This is because although the true lead of real knowledge is something primordial, being produced from within the temporal, it carries acquired energy. First one uses real knowledge to control and stabilize conscious knowledge, not letting conscious knowledge fly off outside; once conscious knowledge is stabilized, it is necessary to gradually remove the acquired pollutant energy carried by this real knowledge, so that eventually none is left at all. Only then is the elixir perfected. If any of that acquired energy is not extracted, not removed, conscious knowledge cannot become a round and bright jewel. When you take out one part of pollutant energy in real knowledge, you add one part of pure energy to conscious knowledge; when you take out one hundred percent of the polluted energy in real knowledge, you add one hundred percent pure energy to conscious knowledge. When polluted energy is exhausted and pure energy is stable, the firing is done and energy is sufficient; only then do you have the complete luminous jewel of real consciousness, round and bright, and nothing else.

Our author's *Understanding Reality* says, "When you use lead, do not use ordinary lead; and when you have finished using the true lead, that too is thrown away. This is the real secret of using lead. Using lead and not using it—these are veracious words." This is the meaning of extracting lead and adding mercury.

In essence, the work of extracting and adding is none other than the function of warding off danger; extracting and adding are precisely that whereby to ward off danger. Avoiding danger, extracting and adding, being careful for the ten months, not deviating from the correct process, how could the gold elixir not form?

As for the "thirty thousand intervals," it is not that there really is a period of ten months; it is just a metaphor for the process from the restoration of the elixir to the perfection of the elixir, when the spiritual embryo reaches complete maturity. Students should investigate the reality and not destroy the meaning by taking the words literally.

20
WHEN HUSBAND AND WIFE MATE,
CLOUDS AND RAIN FORM IN THE SECRET ROOM.
IN A YEAR THEY GIVE BIRTH TO A CHILD,
AND EACH RIDES ON A CRANE.

The foregoing sections told of the medicines, the firing process, and the power of practice, in each case using similes from alchemy.

The author feared that students would not understand the profound subtlety therein and would mistakenly enter the circuitous routes of auxiliary methods, so he added this section, using the ordinary relationship of man and woman, husband and wife, which is obvious and easy to see, as a metaphor to instruct people.

In the path of cultivating reality, the thousand classics and ten thousand texts just teach people to harmonize yin and yang, to cause yin and yang to merge and return to one energy. Observe how in the world husband and wife meet; when they mate, then they can produce a child. In cultivation of the Tao, yin and yang meet, and then when they mate, they can produce an immortal.

Our real knowledge is yang within yin; this is the "husband." Our conscious knowledge is yin within yang; this is the "wife." After the primal yang in people culminates, acquired conditioning takes over affairs, and the real gets lost outside, as though it lived in another house and did not belong to oneself. Though one may have conscious knowledge, the wife does not see the husband; yin being without the balance of yang, this consciousness has falsehood in it. If the husband, real knowledge, is recognized and called back home to meet the wife, conscious knowledge, and taken into the privacy of the secret room, the husband loves the wife and the wife loves the husband; husband and wife mate, sense and essence combine, so the primal energy comes forth from within nothingness and congeals into the spiritual embryo. Then, adding the work of ten months of incubation, when the energy is replete and the spirit complete, it emerges from the womb; there is a body outside the body, transcending yin and yang, untrammeled by natural process.

Then one goes on to advanced practice, again setting up the furnace and crucible, to carry on the subtle path of nondoing. The child gives birth to grandchildren, and the grandchildren also branch out, producing a thousand changes, ten thousand transformations. Each soars into the skies riding a crane, becoming immortals of the empyrean.

This path is entirely the Tao of yin and yang; giving birth to people and giving birth to immortals is not apart from yin and yang; the only difference is in whether the product is an immortal or an ordinary person. As the immortal San-feng put it, going along with the usual course of conditioning makes one an ordinary person, and going against it makes one an immortal; it is all a matter of reversing the process. The method of reversal cannot be known without a teacher. One who knows can form the elixir in a short time and need not spend three years nurturing it and nine years maturing it. But it is necessary to recognize the true yin and the true yang.

The foregoing explanation has been divided into sections, omitting nothing of the meaning. Now, based on the lines of the original text, also according to the same sectioning, I present verses for explanatory notes, simply phrased but inclusive in meaning, cutting through the metaphors and images, to let students understand at a glance and be further able to comprehend the true interpretation without getting involved in speculation. Then most of the secret of cultivating reality can be grasped.

EXPLANATORY VERSES

1

True intent arouses real knowledge;
Conscious knowledge also spontaneously responds.
The three join as one,
And at once body and mind are settled.

2

The empty room produces light;
In quietude yang is restored:
Gather it and diligently refine it,
Transforming it into violet-gold frost.

3

In the spiritual opening the light of wisdom arises;
Essence appears, and feelings about objects vanish.
Clear and bright the jewel that glows in the dark;
Everywhere is bright and clean.

4

Volatility transmutes into true essence;
The human mind changes into the mind of Tao.
Without refinement by the spiritual fire,
How can gold be separated from the ore?

5

Real knowledge and conscious knowledge;
These two are originally the same energy.
Subjected to refinement by fire,
They merge without a trace of defect.

6

In the occult opening real consciousness appears;
Take the opportunity to get to work to nurture it.
When essence and sense cleave to one another,
They always produce the material for the elixir.

7

There is an opening of open awareness
Which is called the opening of the mysterious female;
Therein are stored spirit and energy,
Originally the root of the celestial and earthly souls.

8

Conscious knowledge is the vitality within fire;
Real knowledge is the jewel within water.
When negativity within water and fire vanishes,
The light is brilliant, truly sound.

9

The spiritual remedy is inherent in oneself;
What is the need to seek it outside?

Preserve the responsiveness of constant shining,
And everywhere you go becomes a forest of jewels.

10

Real knowledge is all real,
But it needs to be espoused by conscious knowledge.
Refining away the yin of acquired conditioning,
The two become one whole.

11

Conscious knowledge likes to wander outside
And needs to be governed by real knowledge;
When the "wife" follows the "husband,"
Water and fire balance each other.

12

Thunder, lake, water, and fire
Are symbols of vitality, spirit, sense, and essence;
If you know how to aggregate them,
You walk alone atop the mountains of the immortals.

13

The firing process is not related to hour or season;
Why bother to seek midnight and noon, winter and summer?
Bathing is washing the dusty mind;
How can spring and autumn govern it?

14

"Metal" sense and "wood" essence
Should not be unbalanced or disparate.
The two are as the same energy;
The spiritual root blooms of itself.

15

So great as to enfold space,
Yet small as a grain of rice;
If you ask about this root source,
It is the one reality alone.

16

The vitalities of heaven and earth, sun and moon,
Are fundamentally inherent in our bodies.
If reality and consciousness do not stray from each other,
Creation is always in the palm of your hand.

17

When essence arises, sense comes to stabilize it;
When sense arises, essence goes to lead it.
When their conflict and struggle are ended,
Then, as of yore, they are unconditioned.

18

Essence and sense merge;
Real and conscious knowledge join.
With fierce refinement and gentle cooking,
A crystal-clear temple is produced.

19

Controlling the mind is called bathing;
Incubation involves extraction and addition.
At every moment, forestall danger;
As accomplishment deepens, you naturally enter the mystery.

20

When you understand the principle of yin and yang,
The spiritual embryo is not hard to form;
Producing a child, also producing grandchildren,
Eternal life never ends.

Each section of this classic text on the essence of alchemy is
sound; each line points to reality. The furnace and crucible, medicinal substances, firing process, order of practical cultivation, doing
and nondoing, from start to finish, are all included. Although the
text is brief, it contains the overall meaning of the whole text of
Understanding Reality.

Now I have explained the symbols and metaphors in this text, breaking open the core to see the nucleus, splitting the bones to reveal the marrow, in order to shed some light for beginning students to guide them into the right path. But I fear that students may not know how actually to put it into practice and, not consummating the task of a student, may develop false imaginations about the great Tao and seek at random, deceiving themselves about the path ahead. So here, after having made these explanatory notes on the text, I also add Twenty-four Essentials for Students and Twenty-four Secrets of Alchemy. I phrase them very simply, so that what they refer to may be easily recognized, thereby bringing to light the secrets of which the ancient teachers did not speak.

If people of determination can use these essentials and secrets to study and understand the text itself, proceeding in order, then those who study the Tao will eventually understand the Tao, and those who practice the Tao will eventually accomplish the Tao. It is to be hoped that people will not waste the months and years rushing into byways.

TWENTY-FOUR ESSENTIALS FOR STUDENTS

1

See through things of the world.
If you cannot see through the things of the world,
You will sink into an ocean of suffering. How can you get out?

2

Cut off entanglements.
If you cannot cut off entanglements,
The vicious cycles of compulsive habit stand before you.

3

Thoroughly investigate principle and meaning.
If you do not know how to discern the principles of body and
    mind,
You cannot distinguish aberration and sanity, and miss the road.

4

Find a teacher and associates.

When you empty the mind, you can fill the belly;
If you are self-satisfied, you will grow old without development.

5

Make determination endure.

If you want to accomplish something that endures unchanging,
It requires work that endures unceasing.

6

Get rid of anger and hatred.

If you do not sweep yourself clean of anger and hatred,
You will be full of turbulence, which will obscure the truth.

7

Relinquish attachment to the physical body.

See the physical body as something temporary and artificial,
And naturally there will be a way to seek the real body.

8

Do not be afraid of hard work.

With strength of mind, one will be able to climb to the summit;
If you are afraid of hardship, you will never enter the real.

9

Tolerate ignominy and endure dishonor.

Tolerate ignominy, and though lowly you cannot be surpassed;
Endure dishonor, and through yielding you can be strong.

10

Forgive people and defer to others.

It is essential to humble oneself and honor others;
Equanimous deference is a good method.

11

Take possessions lightly; take life seriously.

Ask yourself—even if you pile up mountains of gold,
Can you buy off impermanence?

12

View others and self as the same.

Others and self have the same source, without high or low;
If you discriminate between "them" and "us," you raise dust.

13

Do not be deluded by alcohol or sex.

If you do not drink, your nature will not be deranged;
If you are chaste, your life force will be stable.

14

Accept hunger and cold as they come.

Dressing and eating according to circumstances, stop idle
imagination;
If you are afraid of hunger and cold, your will won't be firm.

15

Leave life and death to destiny.

Two things, death and life, depend entirely on nature;
The one will to seek the Way is always up to oneself.

16

Do whatever you can to be helpful.

Wherever you are, continue to perform worthy deeds;
Seeing danger, exert your utmost power to help people.

17

Do not take a liking to excitement.

It is easy to lose the real in the midst of excitement and glamour;
In the realms of the senses you can derange your essential nature.

18

Do not be proud or complacent.

Arrogance arouses the hatred of others;
If you are self-satisfied, you cannot bear the Tao.

19

Do not crave fine food.

Superior people plan for the Way, not for food;
Inferior people nurture the palate, not the mind.

20

Do not talk about right and wrong.

Everyone should sweep the snow from his own door
And not be concerned about the frost on another's roof.

21

Do not use intellectual brilliance.

If you have talent, do not employ it; always be as if inept;
If you have knowledge, hide it, appearing to be ignorant.

22

Sleep less and work more.

Working by day, cautious by night, effort never ceasing,
Giving up sleep, forgetting to eat, the will must be firm.

23

Do not take a liking to fine things.

Pearls and jade, gold and silver, are things outside the body;
Vitality and spirit, essence and life, are the fundamental
    treasures.

24

Be consistent from beginning to end.

If you work without strength, it is hard to reach deep attainment;
Only when you die embracing the Tao do you see reality.

These twenty-four essentials are important passageways for students which must be put into actual practice. When you have passed through each one and applied them in your life, only then can you meet a real teacher and hear about the great Tao. If there is even one that you cannot practice and get through, even if you meet a real teacher and hear about the Tao, it is not certain to benefit you.

The teacher's function is to polish away errors, to clearly perceive and subtly test the student and see whether the student is genuine or false. A genuine, sincere person is like real gold, which has no fear of fire, become brighter the more it is refined in the fire, being appraised by an expert, certified and accepted.

Someone without will may start out diligently but eventually slacks off; outwardly obedient yet inwardly refractory, such people will greedily fantasize about the treasures of others without being able to carry out their own tasks. This is what is called not getting rid of temper, not changing the attitude, falling into the sea of vicious circles; even if you accumulate vast hordes of gold and jade, the spirits and immortals will laugh coldly and will not respond. Such people cannot even hear the Way, much less accomplish it.

Those who hear the Way are small sages; those who accomplish the Way are great sages. The affair of great sages is certainly not within the capabilities of empty obscurantists.

TWENTY-FOUR SECRETS OF ALCHEMY

I

Repair the alchemical workshop.
Nourish the temporal; strengthen the physical body.
To nourish the temporal is the point of departure;
When vitality, energy, and spirit are vigorous, one can bear
    hunger and cold.
Having cultivated the physical body until it is firm and strong,

Giving shelter from the rain and wind, it is good for refining the
elixir.

2

Refine the self and set up the foundation.

Overcome anger and lust; conquer the self and return to
normalcy.

Refining the self and mastering the mind are building the
foundation;
Mundane feelings and idle thoughts are all to be thrown away.
When you have refined your self to where it does not exist,
You are imperturbable and unshakable, and cannot be deluded
by things.

3

Set up the crucible and furnace.

Stabilize the will with firmness; do the work with flexibility.

Making the will firm and strong is setting up the crucible;
Gradually progressing in the work is setting up the furnace.
Firmness and flexibility are both used, without imbalance;
Having prepared, work the fire and the convergence according to
the time.

4

Cull the medicines.

Seek the real in the artificial; pick the gold out of sand.

The great medicines are three—vitality, energy, spirit;
It is necessary first to distinguish the true from the false.
The division between right and wrong is slight;
Be careful not to mix them up.

5

Use lead to control mercury.

When real knowledge is not obscured, conscious knowledge is
not flighty.

Another name for sense is true lead;

Essence, light and mercuric, is represented as mercury.
When you understand the method of bringing sense to stabilize
essence,
The human mentality does not arise and the mind of Tao is
complete.

6
The yellow woman harmonizes.
When true intent does not scatter, yin and yang naturally
harmonize.

You should know that the true intent is the "yellow woman";
Truthfulness alone can harmonize the four forms,
Aggregating the five elements uses its power;
Perfecting the being and building life are not apart from it.

7
Lead and mercury intermingle.
Essence goes to seek sense; sense comes back to essence.

Putting the lead in the mercury, sense returns to essence;
Putting the mercury in the lead, essence cleaves to sense.
When sense and essence merge without obstruction,
There is no worry that the great Way will not be accomplished.

8
Work the fire to smelt and refine.
Activate sane energy; sweep out aberrant energy.

Gentle cooking and fierce refinement are the methods of
immortals;
Fire comes forth in the spiritual furnace, yin and yang,
Burning away the thousand kinds of pollutants.
Naturally the great medicines emanate misty light.

9
The restored elixir congeals.
Firmness and flexibility balance each other; essence and sense are
as one.

When essence and sense are unified, that is called the restored
    elixir;
Bright and clear, reality and consciousness join into one whole.
Having obtained the original priceless jewel,
Carefully guard it; practice observation of the spirit.

10

Bathe and incubate.

Do not let thoughts arise; do not let attention scatter.

Washing off defilement and dust is the method of bathing;
Do not be negligent, do not be forceful, join yin and yang.
When entanglements do not arise, the basis of the elixir is stable;
Nurturing the spiritual root, the flower buds are fragrant.

11

The basis of the elixir becomes mature.

Within black there is white; when quietude culminates, there is
    movement.

Within black there is white—the herb of long life.
Within darkness is concealed light—the life-prolonging tonic.
Refining it into something crystal-clear and pure,
It penetrates heaven and earth with a ray of light.

12

Ingest the gold elixir.

Gather the spirit into the room, transmuting earthliness.

The elixir ingested does not come from outside;
The refined real consciousness rests within.
The internal organs produce light; earthly energy is transmuted;
Without confusion or obscurity, obstacles are broken through.

13

Move the furnace and crucible.

The root source in hand, plant and nurture according to the time.

The gold elixir in hand, there is true transmission;
Moving the furnace and crucible is a mystery within mystery.

Henceforth carefully cook the great medicine,
Refining the primordial within the primordial opening.

14

Congeal the spiritual embryo.

All the spirit gathered, the five elements merge.

The five energies return to the origin and gather on the spiritual
    pedestal;
The primordial seed is already firmly planted.
As though an idiot, as though drunk, as though deep asleep,
In ecstasy and profound abstraction you congeal the spiritual
    embryo.

15

Difficulty in the morning, darkness at night.

Know the male, keep the female; refine with the natural fire.

Knowing the male, it is also necessary to keep the female.
Steaming with water and fire is not a matter of the hour.
There is naturally a pivot which turns over the trigrams;
What is the need to make conscious effort?

16

Incubate the embryo.

Like a hen sitting on an egg, like an oyster embracing a pearl.

Concentrate single-mindedly, like a hen sitting on an egg;
Be thoroughly sincere, like an oyster embracing a pearl.
Hour after hour quietly watch over the aperture of open
    awareness,
To avoid letting water and fire be isolated in the furnace.

17

Forestall danger.

Externally oblivious of the body, internally oblivious of the mind.

Before celestial energy is thoroughly pure, there is still danger;
As long as earthly energy is not exhausted, it is necessary to
    prevent peril.

If the pollution of acquired conditioning is dissolved away,
It can be guaranteed that the embryo will not be damaged.

18

In ten months the embryo is mature.
Primordial energy is pure; conditioning is evaporated.

After ten months of work, the embryo is finally mature;
When conditioning is all dissolved, the primal is complete.
Utterly pure and clean, there is nothing else;
It is one naturalness, neither form nor void.

19

Wait for the time to break free.
No thought, no doing, not obsessed, not indifferent.

Basically there is a time to break free, transformed;
It will not do to be too early or too late.
Truthfulness within reaches outside, not admitting force;
When a melon is ripe, it naturally separates from the stem.

20

The infant emerges.
Breaking through nondifferentiation, leaping into nothingness.

Keep still in the yellow court and nurture the valley spirit;
With body complete and energy replete, the fire is stopped—
With a peal of thunder, the gate of heaven opens,
And out leaps the indestructible immortal person.

21

Breast-feed for three years.
Enlightened but not shining, illumined but not using it.   ·

When real consciousness is refined into a golden body,
It never ever falls into the dust.
Nursing it for three years, enlightened but not shining,
Knowing before and understanding after, the sage is spiritual.

22

Exiting and entering at will.

Body and spirit both sublimated, merging into reality with
   the Tao.

Body and spirit both sublimated, equal to space,

Merging in reality with the Tao, all things are penetrated.

Appearing, hiding, going against or along, no one can fathom it;

Clustered, there is form; dispersed, the wind.

23

Facing a wall for nine years.

Neither being nor nonbeing stand; the universe is ultimately
   empty.

Nine years facing a wall, who is there that knows?

The work of entering the room does not depend on thought.

The universe returns to emptiness; ordinary and holy are gone;

In the realm of silent serenity, the abode of immortals is built.

24

The child also produces grandchildren.

Transformation without end, unfathomable spiritual wonders.

The child also produces grandchildren; ordinary and sage are the
   same—

The only distinction is in going along or coming back in reverse.

Ancient immortals left the secret of a great elixir,

With endless transmutations, getting through everywhere.

These twenty-four secrets are steps of the process which must be
thoroughly understood, as the slightest deviation produces a great
miss. Since ancient times the immortals and real people usually
have not clearly indicated the order of the process; concealing the
mother and speaking of the children, they have just instructed
people by means of metaphors and symbols, fearing pilferage by
unsuitable people.

Since I have received spoken instruction from a teacher, at the risk of making a mistake I wish to reveal this teaching publicly to those who aspire to it. Even if one lacks the power to put it into practice, simply getting to hear about the great Way is a measureless blessing.

But such a great task requires people of great strength to carry it out; it also requires people to have great character in order to perform it. If one has great strength but lacks great character, there are likely to arise obstacles that will prevent accomplishment of the great Way.

Therefore, if one wants to traverse this path, one should first build character. For mediocre and lesser people, character is more important than the path, because if their virtue is not great, even if they can hear about the Way they cannot necessarily attain it. Students of the Tao should first recognize clearly what these topics mean, know the beginning and the end, when to hurry and when to relax; only then will they have certain insight and avoid wasting effort.

GLOSSARY

Black and white:	Primordial and temporal; non-differentiation and differentiation; transcendence and immanence; detachment and involvement. *See also* Female and male.
Entering the room:	Advanced attainment.
Facing a wall:	Practicing equanimity.
Female and male:	Receptivity and creativity; tranquillity and action.
Gate of heaven:	In psychophysical Taoist yoga, the center of the top of the head, the "opening" from which the spirit is projected; metaphysically, the apex

of consciousness, through which one passes into enlightenment.

Steaming:
Permeation of the being with the combination of "water" and "fire." (See the introduction and text for the significations of water and fire and their combination.)

Turning over the trigrams:
In the unregenerate human being, the order of the water and fire trigrams is thus:

FIRE ☲ Conscious knowledge: tends to "fly up," become dissociated from true reality.

WATER ☵ Real knowledge: tends to "flow off," remain unconscious and inaccessible.

For enlightenment, these are "turned over" or "inverted":

☵ Real knowledge controls conscious knowledge.

☲ Conscious knowledge rises to real knowledge.

Valley spirit:
Open awareness.

Yellow court:
In psychophysical Taoist yoga, the center of the torso; metaphysically, the "center" in the sense of intent (as the force that unifies the being), truthfulness, balance, faith.

Part Two

Solving Symbolic Language

ON SYMBOLIC LANGUAGE

The ancient classics on the science of cultivating reality often speak of the path of nondoing, but seldom speak of the path of doing. However, on the path of nondoing, only those of superior knowledge become suddenly enlightened and attain complete comprehension, understanding everything in one realization, immediately ascending into the realm of sages. Mediocre and lesser people, those who are dull, deeply conditioned, and lacking perceptivity, will find that their power is insufficient to practice the path of nondoing; they will not be able to transcend all objects and reach the goal directly.

During the latter Han dynasty (second century C.E.) Wei Po-yang, a Taoist adept, composed the *Triplex Unity* (*Ts'an t'ung ch'i*) to guide those of middling and lesser faculties. He used images to present the imageless, used forms to allude to the formless. This was the beginning of the term *gold elixir* and the technical symbolism of lead and mercury, sand and silver, raven and rabbit, dragon and tiger, the baby, the girl, medicinal substances, the furnace and cauldron, cooking and refining, and so on.

Later on, many real people who had attained the Tao composed alchemical treatises, all based on the *Triplex Unity*, to expound the subtle principles. Their intention was for students in later times to use the former to study the latter, and use the latter to understand the former.

Nevertheless, later students did not look into the meanings of the code words and did not figure out the principles of the symbols. Seeing talk of gold elixir, lead, mercury, cauldron, and furnace, they thought it referred to the preparation of potions to ingest, and they took to chemistry. Seeing talk of raven and rabbit, dragon and tiger, they thought it referred to the internal organs, and they took to visualization exercises. Seeing talk of other and self, yin and yang, male and female, they thought it referred to conjugal elixir, and they took to sexual yoga. Seeing talk of going along, reversing, and inverting, they thought it referred to forced effort, and they took to energy circulation practices. Seeing talk of nondoing to cultivate essence, they took it to mean utter quiescence, and they got involved in quietism. Seeing talk of doing to cultivate life, they thought it meant exercise, and came to cling to form. These and other schools arose, all taking a deer to be a horse, taking a crow for a phoenix, not only without benefit to essence and life, but even to the detriment of essence and life. Could this have been the intention of the ancient teachers in using symbolic language?

Symbols are representations, speaking of one thing to allude to something else. To take an example from the field of common knowledge and experience, consider the cooking and brewing of food and drink. The pot is the "cauldron"; the stove is the "furnace." Water is put in the pot; fire is kindled in the stove. The basic tendency of fire is to flame upward, that of water to flow downward; when we put the water in the pot above and the fire in the stove below, water and fire are thus "reversed"—they complement one another, so that the food and drink are cooked and brewed. This represents ordinary water and ordinary fire complementing each other.

The strength in people is impetuous and volatile, so it is associated with fire; flexibility is relaxed and calm, so it is associated with water. Using flexibility to nurture strength, using strength to complete flexibility, strength and flexibility match each other, so that there is neither haste nor dawdling, effecting a return to equipoise, with the result that the Tao is easy to accomplish. This is the principle of the mutual complementarity of psychological water and psychological fire. Using the image of complementarity of ordinary water and fire to represent the principle of complementarity of psychological water and fire, that principle is clear.

Let us consider another example. Suppose a man is originally prosperous, but becomes profligate and squanders his fortune; then, on the verge of destitution, he repents of his errors, struggles and labors for a living again, gradually accumulates substance, and eventually reestablishes his fortune. This symbolizes return to the origin. The vitality, spirit, and sacred energy in the human body are originally complete and full; mixing with temporal conditioning, going along with the process of creation, expends vitality and belabors the spirit, so that the basic energy declines and the source wanes. If, on the verge of exhaustion, one can turn back, quell anger and cupidity, get rid of falsehood and preserve truth, by gradual application of effort one can eventually return to the root and restore life. This is the principle of return to the origin. Using the image of restoration and recovery of a man in the world to represent the principle of return to the origin by practice of Tao, that principle is clear.

To take another example, when a man and a woman mate, they are able to produce children, who produce grandchildren; this represents the continuing birth of the human Tao. When the yin and yang in the human being match and unite, they can produce enlightened adepts; this is the principle of continuing birth in the alchemical Tao. Using the image of continuing birth of the human Tao to represent the principle of continuing birth in the alchemical Tao, that principle is clear.

The alchemical classics all use metaphors to illustrate principles;

they are telling people to discern from the image the principle to be practiced, not to turn away from the principle and act on the image. It is a pity that people do not investigate the principles, only recognizing the images. There are very many symbolic expressions used in alchemical classics; students should proceed from the symbol to discover the principle. When you get the image, forget the words; when you get the intent, forget the image. Then you will be close.

ON GOING ALONG AND REVERSAL

Everyone in the world knows the path of "going along," but not the path of "reverse operation." What is going along? It means going along with natural process. What is reversal? It means reversal of natural process. Going along with natural process gives birth to humans and other beings, the cycle of birth, aging, sickness, and death never ceasing. Reversing the natural process produces enlightened adepts who are neither born nor perish, having a life span equal to that of the universe.

Ordinarily, after people are born, as they grow up they become imbued with temporal conditioning; inwardly, emotions and desires distract them from reality, while outwardly objects and events tax their bodies. They take the false to be real, take the aberrant to be correct, take misery for pleasure; following their desires to any lengths, they deplete their original vitality, energy, and spirit almost to the point of exhaustion, and thoroughly obscure their inherent round and bright true essence, unwilling to stop until they die. Therefore they undergo birth after birth, death after death, sunk for myriad aeons; this is what is called throwing oneself to one's death even without having been called by the king of death.

People of great wisdom reverse the operation of the natural

process; they are not bound by the natural process, not molded by yin and yang, not compelled by myriad things, not changed by myriad conditions. Planting lotuses in a fire, hauling a boat through mud and water, they make temporary use of things of the world to practice the principles of the Tao, by the human Tao completing the celestial Tao. They uproot the mundane senses conditioned by history and sweep away all acquired influences. They rule their own destinies and are not ruled by fate. Restoring the whole, original being, they avoid compulsive routine, transcend all worlds, and become incorruptible.

But this celestial mechanism of practicing reversal in the midst of accord has a secret which is communicated verbally and transmitted mentally; one must seek the guidance of a true teacher, for it cannot be known through arbitrary guesswork. Students all over the world use their own meager light and narrow views, memorize a few sayings, ponder a few mystical stories, and think they know the Tao; seeking no further for guidance, they become charlatans, self-appointed preachers who are blind themselves and take in others who are blind. It is wrong to do this.

There are also mixed-up people who cannot recognize true teachers and go from one imbecile to another learning a few minor techniques and imagine they have the Tao; then, when enlightened people appear before them, they are unwilling to humble themselves to learn. They perform various practices at random: some consider descent of the energy in the heart and ascent of the energy in the genitals to be the practice of reversal; some consider the circulation of energy up the spine and down the front of the body to be the practice of reversal; some consider sending the vitality up to boost the brain to be the practice of reversal; some consider holding the breath and steadying the spirit to be the practice of reversal; some consider taking sexual energy from women to vitalize men to be the practice of reversal; some consider having the man below and the woman above to be the practice of reversal. There are thousands of such methods; they are all contrary to the path of sages and are not reverse operation of the natural process. They are all ways to death, not to life.

What such people do not realize is that reversal means going back to the origin of life. It is like someone who has left home and gone far away turning around and returning home. Although it is called reverse action, in fact it is action in accord with principle, so it is great accord within reversal. It is called reversal because it goes contrary to the course of action of ordinary people. Those who have taken to auxiliary methods, with all their intricacies, have been confused by the word *reversal* and have come to do all sorts of practices in the physical sphere. In the end they will fall into emptiness. Is this not foolish?

ON THE MEDICINES

When the alchemical classics and writings of the masters speak of gathering medicines and refining gold elixir, they are referring to primordial, formless, immaterial realities, not to mundane, physical, material medicines and not to substances in the human body.

After people are born, they accept the false and lose the real, expending their naturally complete treasure to the point of exhaustion, so that the body becomes pure mundanity, full of aberrant energies, as if afflicted with a serious illness, death being just a matter of time. Because of this, if not for genuine effective "medicine," they have no way to restore the mundane to the celestial and preserve essence and life.

What is genuine effective medicine? It is primordial, true, unified energy; it is primordial vitality, energy, and spirit, the "three treasures." The primordial, true, unified energy is also called true seed. It does not descend into material form; it is ultimate nonbeing yet contains ultimate being, is ultimate emptiness yet contains ultimate fulfillment. Truly empty yet subtly existing, it governs the three treasures of vitality, energy, and spirit.

The three treasures are also not physical things but formless realities. As an ancient adept said, the vitality is not sexual vitality, the energy is not metabolic energy, the spirit is not the thinking mind. Though they are three, the treasures all return to one primordial energy; the three combine into one energy, the one energy differentiates into three.

Gathering medicines means gathering these three treasures of one energy; operating the fire of reality to refine them, one produces elixir which transmutes all mundane energies in a person, returning to unadulterated celestial energy, the pure, undefiled original being. It is like a person with an illness using medicine to cure it and become well.

Medicine here is a metaphor, but students in later generations took the alchemical classics literally and thought the medicines were material substances; they gathered herbs in the mountains and compounded them into potions, vainly hoping for long life. Some gathered minerals and cooked them into elixirs, which they ingested, imagining they would thereby become able to fly aloft. What they did not realize was that material medicines can only cure physical ailments and cannot cure immaterial ailments. Immaterial sickness can only be cured by gathering the primordial, true, unified energy.

The *Triplex Unity* says, "It is easy to work with what is of the same species, hard to work with what is not of the same kind." *Understanding Reality* says, "When bamboo breaks, you need bamboo to mend it; if you want to hatch chickens, you need eggs. Whatever is not of the same kind is a waste of effort; how can that compare to true lead combining with the potential for sagehood?" The true lead is precisely this primordial, true, unified energy; all those who take ordinary drugs to be herbs of immortality should wake up when they read this.

ON THE FIRING PROCESS

The "firing process" spoken of in the alchemical classics and writings of the masters is a metaphor for the order of practical spiritual work. Generally speaking, in spiritual work there is that which comes first and that which comes later; there are times for relaxation and hurry, advance and withdrawal. It will not do to put off for later what must be done first, or to do first what must be done later; it will not do to relax when one should hurry, or to hurry when one should relax. It will not do to withdraw when one should advance, or to advance when one should withdraw. It is as when one cooks medicines over a fire, there are times for gentle firing, intense firing, and stopping at sufficiency. So the order of application of effort in cultivation of reality is represented as a "firing process."

However, the firing process of spiritual work is not a matter of years, months, days, or hours; it applies to every moment—doing first what should be done first, doing later what should be done later, hurrying when one should hurry, relaxing when one should relax, advancing when one should advance, withdrawing when one should withdraw, shifting effectively at the appropriate times.

What should be done first is to establish inward discipline; what should be done after that is to deflect externals. When one should hurry is when applying effort; when one should relax is when gently nurturing. When one should advance is when celestial energy is insufficient and should be advanced; when one should withdraw is when mundane energy arises and should be withdrawn.

This is the true principle of the firing process. It is not the yogins' theory of advancing the yang fire at midnight, withdrawing the yin convergence at noon, and bathing at six A.M. and six P.M. It is also not the theory of advancing the yang fire at the winter solstice, withdrawing the yin convergence at the summer solstice, and bathing at the vernal and autumnal equinoxes.

The natural world has its own times, and humans have their own times; the times of the natural world cannot be precisely identified with human times. Winter, summer, spring, fall, midnight, noon, six in the morning, and six in the evening—in the human being, these times are present at every juncture. An ancient classic says, "No need to look for midnight and noon in the sky; there is arising of yang within the body." The arising of yang is midnight / winter solstice; the arising of yin is noon / summer solstice. Yang joining yin is six A.M. / vernal equinox; yin joining yang is six P.M. / autumnal equinox. These are the living times and seasons, not the lifeless times and seasons of the calendar.

The firing process as explained in the sixty-four hexagrams of the *I ching* also indicates the principles of advancement and withdrawal of yin and yang, teaching people to make adjustments according to the situation, adapting effectively in application of effort; it does not teach people to practice according to the sequence of the sixty-four hexagrams. *Understanding Reality* says, "Setting up symbols in the hexagrams is based on descriptions of the modes; understanding the symbol, forget the words—the idea is clear of itself. The whole world is astray, only clinging to symbols, acting out the energies of the hexagrams in hopes of flying aloft."

When reading such books, you should understand the ancients' intent in choosing symbols and making verbal formulations; once the meaning is realized, the symbol can be forgotten. The thousands of books on the path of cultivating reality are all in symbolic language; though the images they choose are not the same, they are all used to clarify yin and yang, going along and reversing, the medicines, real and false, and the order of the firing process. They do not talk about anything other than this.

Since I have truly understood the meanings in the symbols through the guidance of teachers, I dare not keep this knowledge to myself and want to make it public, for those of discernment. Therefore I have taken essential points from the alchemical classics and produced diagrams to communicate their reality, analyzing and clarifying right and wrong to resolve students' doubts. The rest may be deduced by analogy.

1. *The State in the Womb*

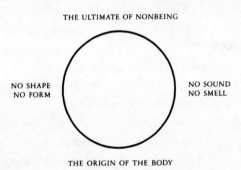

THE ULTIMATE OF NONBEING

NO SHAPE
NO FORM

NO SOUND
NO SMELL

THE ORIGIN OF THE BODY

Before one's parents give birth to one's body, when the yin and yang energies of male and female interact, in the midst of darkness there is a point of living potential, which comes forth from nothing. This is what is called the primordial, true, unified generative energy. This energy enters into the sperm and ovum, fusing them into one: formless, it produces form; immaterial, it produces substance. The internal organs, the organs of sense, and the various parts of the body evolve, all becoming complete naturally. Even the mother who carries the unborn child does not know how this happens as it does.

Inexperienced students, unaware of this principle, imagine that when people are in the womb their umbilical cord conveys the mother's breath, so that the fetus exhales when the mother exhales and inhales when the mother inhales, gradually evolving and forming. This is not so. Respiration is acquired energy; how can acquired energy cause the sperm and ovum to evolve into a body? And how could breath enter into the womb? What they do not realize is that in the mother's womb there is only the primal point of generative energy, undifferentiated, which first causes the embryo to congeal, then nurtures the embryo, and eventually causes it to become complete. The whole process is accomplished by this generative energy, with nothing else mixed in.

At this point, though there is the human form, there is no human way; nothing in the world, not even water, fire, or weapons, can harm one here. Emotions and desires cannot reach one here. Ultimately, in reality there is just openness alone. When the ancient immortals taught people to practice the Tao to return to what they were like before their parents gave birth to them, they meant returning to the state of openness, beyond sense. Where there is no sense is the ultimate of nonbeing. The ultimate of nonbeing is the extreme of nothingness, where there is only nonbeing.

2. The State of the Infant

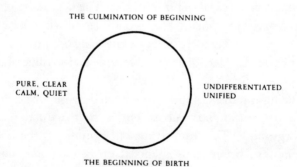

THE CULMINATION OF BEGINNING

PURE, CLEAR
CALM, QUIET

UNDIFFERENTIATED
UNIFIED

THE BEGINNING OF BIRTH

After ten months in the womb, the fetus is fully developed; like a ripe melon falling off the stem, the fetus breaks out of the amnion and emerges, feet toward the sky and head toward the earth. With a cry the infant first comes in contact with the air, breathing it in so that it mixes with the primordial original energy within. The primordial is the body; the temporal is the function. The temporal depends on the primordial to breathe in and out, while the primordial depends on the temporal to nurture the vascular system.

Furthermore, at the moment of that cry, the conscious spirit of the generations of history also enters into the opening and merges with the primordial original spirit. The original spirit depends on the conscious spirit to subsist, while the conscious spirit depends on the original spirit for effective awareness.

Nevertheless, though the newborn infant has acquired energy and acquired spirit, still the primordial governs the temporal and the temporal obeys the primordial. The primordial and the temporal merge into nondifferentiation; without discrimination or cognition, there is one reality alone.

When the ancient immortals taught people to find out the point of birth, they meant to find out the beginning of birth which is to find out the appearance of the infant. Deluded people, not knowing this, have erroneously said that "the point of birth" means the woman's birth canal. This is wrong. The beginning of birth, the appearance of the infant, means pure clarity, without blemish; this is the germ and embryo of sages, the root and sprout of immortals and buddhas. Here one is ungraspable and invulnerable, because one is mindless.

Being mindless, one is not hindered by birth and death; there are no calamities, no troubles. This is the image of the culmination of beginning. The culmination of beginning is the final limit of beginning, before getting mixed up in temporal conditioning. Though merged with the temporal, it is the primordial alone which controls things. This is because it is at the culmination of beginning; it is beginning as it springs from nonbeing.

3. *The State of the Child*

CULMINATION OF THE GREAT

NOT FORM
NOT VOID

NO EGO
NO DESIRE

UNITY OF PRIMORDIAL AND TEMPORAL

After a person has grown from infancy to the point where he can walk, speak, and follow others' directions, he is called a child. The infant has no discrimination or cognition, but the child already has discrimination and cognition, so it is as if floating clouds are dotting the sky. Having discrimination and cognition derives from the culmination of beginning eventually reaching the culmination of the great. The culmination of the great means the limit of the universal, which must be followed by the arising of the particular; when yang culminates, it must shift to yin. At this moment, however, the particular has not yet come, yin has not yet arisen; it is still the primordial that does things, while the acquired is latent. Though there is discrimination and cognition, the encrustation of the faculties has not yet taken place and acquired influences have not yet invaded; when hungry, one just eats, and when cold, one just puts on clothes. Joy, anger, sadness, and happiness come and go, vanishing as they arise; one does not know about differences of wealth and status, but is spontaneous and has no extraneous thoughts.

This, too, is the germ and embryo of sages, the root and sprout of immortals and buddhas. The ignorant consider the child to be the infant, but this is wrong. They both are imbued with natural reality, but they are different in terms of state, the infant being higher and the child lower, and they are also different in terms of intellectual knowledge, which the infant does not have but the child does. Therefore, to represent return to the origin, the ancient immortals chose the fundamental aspect of the infant and not the naive aspect of the child.

4. *Yin and Yang Divide*

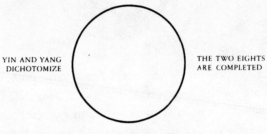

YIN AND YANG
DICHOTOMIZE

THE TWO EIGHTS
ARE COMPLETED

THE APERTURE OF AWARENESS OPENS
GOOD AND BAD DIVIDE

After people grow from childhood to the point where the energies of the two eights are complete, yang culminates and yin arises, opening an aperture; yin and yang divide, each dwelling on one side. Then there is artificiality within the real; here intellectual knowledge gradually develops, and good and bad are discriminated. This is the division of the culmination of the universal, dichotomizing yin and yang.

The completion of the energies of the two eights is like the upper and lower crescents of the moon joining into one shining orb, which symbolizes the culmination of primordial yang, like the culmination of the great, the culmination of the universal. When yang culminates, it must turn to yin, as when the universal culminates, unity divides into yin and yang, which separate as two.

The ignorant take such talk of two eights and production of yin to mean a boy's emission of yin vitality (semen) at the age of sixteen. This is wrong. Considering how some boys emit semen at fourteen or fifteen, some at sixteen or seventeen, and some at eighteen or nineteen, since there is no set age for this, we know that the two eights refer not to people's age but to the fullness of energy.

5. *The Five Elements Separate*

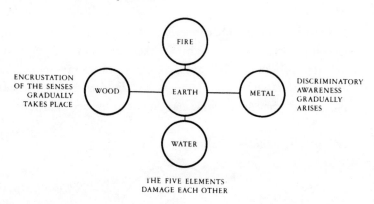

THE FIVE ELEMENTS
DAMAGE EACH OTHER

Once yin and yang divide, the five elements also become aberrated. The five elements—metal, wood, water, fire, and earth—represent sense, essence, vitality, spirit, and energy. In the primal state, these elements foster one another in harmonious union and are manifested in action as the five virtues of benevolence, justice, courtesy, wisdom, and truthfulness.

In the conditioned state, the five elements are imbalanced and damage each other; this manifests in action as the five rebels of joy, anger, sadness, happiness, and desire.

When the five elements are united, the five virtues are present and yin and yang are one. When the five elements are fragmented, the five rebels rise up and yin and yang are confused.

Once the five elements separate, discriminatory awareness gradually arises, and the encrustation of the senses gradually takes place; the real retreats and the artificial assumes authority. Now even the state of the child is lost.

The ignorant assign the five elements variously to five internal organs, but this is wrong. The five internal organs, having form and substance, are inns for the conditioned five elements, not the gardens of virtues of the primal five elements. If you identify the five organs with the five elements, how can the five organs divide and unite?

The five elements differ in being either primal or conditioned; the primal originate before birth, the conditioned emerge after birth. The primal produce sages, the conditioned produce ordinary people. Though the five elements are divided into primal and conditioned, they are all alive and do not have fixed positions.

6. *Acquired Conditioning Runs Affairs*

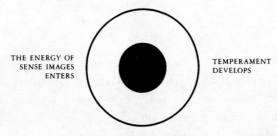

THE ENERGY OF SENSE IMAGES ENTERS

TEMPERAMENT DEVELOPS

YIN IS PRODUCED WITHIN YANG

Yin and yang divided, the five elements separated, once conditioning mixes in, the primordial retreats; at this point the acquired temperament emerges, and external impacts come and condition the senses, which then beckon emotions and desires. Pristine purity is gradually invaded by mundane energy. Once mundane energy enters, it gradually grows, and celestial energy gradually wanes away. Indulgently pursuing desires, one eventually becomes totally subservient to them.

The ignorant think that the temperament is the real nature, but this is not so. The real nature is the nature as divinely decreed and belongs to the primordial; this is beneficial to people. The temperament is the nature created by people and emerges from acquired conditioning; this is harmful to people. How can acquired nature be identified with primal nature?

7. *Pure Mundanity, Nothing Celestial*

POSITIVITY VANISHES   NEGATIVITY IS NOT TOTAL

WHEN THE OIL IS USED UP, THE LAMP GOES OUT

WHEN THE MARROW IS EXHAUSTED, THE PERSON DIES

As acquired conditioning runs affairs, mundanity increases and the celestial retreats, day after day, year after year. Inwardly, myriad thoughts cause trouble; outwardly, myriad things coerce. Under inward and outward attack, the celestial energy wanes away and the whole being becomes totally mundane; as the three treasures are depleted, the life forces cannot be sustained, and death is inevitable.

Ignorant people think that when they end their days and die is a matter of fate, but this is not so. What human life depends on is positive energy; as long as any positive energy at all remains, one does not die. And as long as negative energy is incomplete, one does not die. If one goes along and lets the negative mundane energy extinguish the positive celestial energy, this is looking for the way to death on one's own—what has it got to do with fate?

The foregoing seven diagrams represent the process of producing humans, going along with the usual natural process: the next seven represent the process of producing immortals, reversing the usual natural process.

1 . *Refining the Self, Setting Up the Foundation*

QUELLING ANGER
AND CUPIDITY

CONQUERING THE SELF
RETURNING TO ORDER

PURGING DEFILEMENT, ELIMINATING FALSEHOOD
KEEPING TRUTHFULNESS

The path of cultivating reality is the path of restoration and return. Restoration means causing the self which has gone to come back; return means regaining the celestial positivity which has been lost. This means restoration and return of the original, real celestial positivity in the midst of total mundanity.

Once people's conditioning runs affairs, they become totally mundane, so the primordial celestial energy wanes away to the verge of exhaustion. Without the work of restoration, how can that which is lacking be recovered, how can that which is lost be regained?

The work of restoration begins with refining the self and setting up the foundation. Refining the self means burning away temporal accretions encrusting the senses, temperamental biases, and all acquired energies with which one has become imbued by habituation. This means quelling anger and cupidity, conquering the self, and returning to order.

If one can quell anger and cupidity, conquer oneself, and return to order, one will be free from wishful thinking and rumination, and will be imperturbable and unwavering. This fundamental stability is like the necessity of building a foundation first when you build a house; when the foundation is strong and stable, it will be able to sustain the weight of the house as it is built. So self-refinement is in setting up the foundation; setting up the foundation is not other than self-refinement.

The ignorant think that refining the self means guarding the heart and that setting up the foundation means stopping the flow of semen. This is wrong. The work of self-refinement is only finished when mundanity is ended and the celestial is pure; until this is accomplished, the work cannot be stopped. If one thinks that guarding the heart and stopping the flow of semen are refining the self and setting up the foundation, how will one be able to complete the great work of the gold elixir?

An ancient immortal said, "Restoring the elixir takes place at once; refining the self requires ten months." So we know it is not a matter of guarding the heart and stopping the semen.

2. *The Natural, Innocent True Mind*

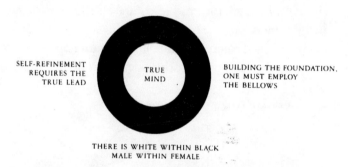

SELF-REFINEMENT REQUIRES THE TRUE LEAD

TRUE MIND

BUILDING THE FOUNDATION, ONE MUST EMPLOY THE BELLOWS

THERE IS WHITE WITHIN BLACK
MALE WITHIN FEMALE

Refining the self and setting up the foundation are not a matter of forced control, forced effort, or austere practices. What the work requires is first to recognize the natural, innocent true mind, and then to use this true mind to refine the self. Then a point of celestial energy emerges within the darkness; this is called true consciousness. When the true consciousness appears, right and wrong, false and true, are distinctly clear; one will not be compelled by desire for things and will not be influenced by sense objects, so self-refinement is very easy.

If one cannot find the true mind, then false and true will not be distinguised, right and wrong will not be clear; so even if one uses the mind to control the mind, after all it is the human mind at work, with repression and force. This is what is meant by the saying, "If you try to get rid of errant thoughts, that will increase the ailment; to try to head for reality is also amiss." How can one reach the selfless state in this way?

The ignorant mistake the human mentality for the true mind. This is wrong. The true mind is mindless; only the mindless mind is the naturally innocent mind. With this natural innocent mind, one will have no trouble mastering oneself. The *Hundred Character Inscription* says, "Knowing the original progenitor in action and repose, having no concern, who else do you seek?" San-feng said, "When building the foundation, you should use the bellows; when refining the self, you need the true lead." The original progenitor, the bellows, and the true lead, are all different names for the natural, innocent true mind.

Ah, but is the natural, innocent true mind easy to know? If you know it, then by attaining this one thing, myriad tasks are done.

3. *The Celestial Grows, the Mundane Wanes*

CELESTIAL ENERGY
GRADUALLY GROWS
DAY BY DAY

MUNDANE ENERGY
GRADUALLY WANES
DAY BY DAY

ACTIVATING THE MIND OF TAO
DISSOLVING THE HUMAN MIND

Having found the natural, innocent true mind, the autonomous host sits peacefully in the center. Effort for the Tao decreases daily, while accomplishment increases daily. The celestial energy gradually grows; the force of mundanity gradually wanes. Growing and growing, waning and waning, until there can be no more growth or waning, this is the ultimate accomplishment.

The ignorant think that by sitting quietly, inactive, tranquil, indifferent, empty, the celestial energy will increase of itself and the force of mundanity will decrease of itself. This is wrong. The restored elixir is the restoration of the celestial within the mundane. If you want to restore the celestial by quiet sitting without action and tranquil indifference, how can the celestial return by itself, how can the mundane withdraw by itself?

Understanding Reality says, "Even if you know the cinnabar and lead, if you do not know the firing process, it is useless. It all depends on the power of practice; the slightest deviation, and you will fail to crystallize the elixir." By this we can know the way to foster the celestial and withdraw the mundane.

4. *Assembling the Five Elements*

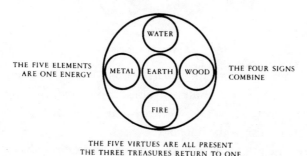

THE FIVE ELEMENTS ARE ONE ENERGY — WATER METAL EARTH WOOD FIRE — THE FOUR SIGNS COMBINE

THE FIVE VIRTUES ARE ALL PRESENT
THE THREE TREASURES RETURN TO ONE

For the celestial to grow and the mundane to wane requires knowledge of assembling the five elements; when the five elements are assembled, the great Tao may be aspired to. The work of assembling is a matter of extracting the primordial five elements from the midst of the conditioned five elements. The conditioned five elements overcome one another, while the primordial five elements foster one another. When the five elements foster one another, they are integrated with the celestial design; this is the five elements as one energy, the combining of the four signs.

Ignorant people think that assembling the five elements means mentally drawing the energies of the heart and genitals up and

ʾown to mix with each other, and conveying the energies of the
ʾr and lungs left and right to join each other. This is wrong. The
ɟies of the internal organs are physical, and whatever is physi-
ɑl is acquired; it becomes, and so also decays. How can this
crystallize the permanent, indestructible jewel of life?

5. *Yin and Yang Merge*

THE EDGE OF THE UNIVERSAL

WITHIN YANG
THERE IS YIN

WITHIN YIN
THERE IS YANG

THE STATE OF THE CHILD

The five elements particularize from within yin and yang.
When the five elements are assembled and united, this means yin
and yang merge into one. When yin and yang merge, the gold
elixir forms; this is the state of the child.

Nevertheless, the energy of acquired conditioning has still not
disappeared. Yet even though the energy of acquired conditioning
has not yet disappeared, since the primordial has been restored,
conditioning submits to it and cannot cause harm. By doing yet
another level of work from this point on, the gold elixir can be
perfected.

The ignorant think that the merging of yin and yang means the
mixing of the heart and genital energies, or the meeting of the
active and passive energy channels, or the intercourse of man and
woman. This is wrong. The gold elixir is made by the crystalliza-
tion of the energy of primordial nothingness; it cannot be formed
by temporal, physical substances.

6. *Unified Energy*

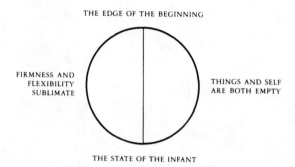

THE EDGE OF THE BEGINNING

FIRMNESS AND
FLEXIBILITY
SUBLIMATE

THINGS AND SELF
ARE BOTH EMPTY

THE STATE OF THE INFANT

When yin and yang return to integral completeness, the state of the child is already restored; from this point on the natural fire of reality operates to burn away residual conditioning and return to the state where there is no discriminatory knowledge, where the spirit is secreted and the energy clusters. This is what is referred to as a man being pregnant, the "fetus" being the state of the infant. This is the point where the living body becomes imbued with energy; this is the edge of the beginning, and it is also called the universal One containing true energy.

Ignorant people think that formation of the spiritual embryo is done by ingesting mineral or vegetable substances. This is wrong. What is formed by ingesting mineral or vegetable substances is no more than clumps of blood or flesh. This only promotes death, and there is no hope of anything else.

7. *Absolutely Open Nothingness*

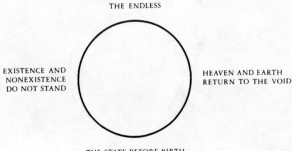

THE ENDLESS

EXISTENCE AND
NONEXISTENCE
DO NOT STAND

HEAVEN AND EARTH
RETURN TO THE VOID

THE STATE BEFORE BIRTH

When the spiritual embryo has formed, then one applies ten months of incubation, the work of gently nurturing it, operating the natural fire of reality to forge and refine it from vagueness to clarity, from weakness to strength. When the cluster of mundanity has been stripped away, the embryo is fully developed, the elixir is done; like a ripe melon dropping off the vine, one suddenly breaks through the undifferentiated, bursts out with the pure spiritual body, leaps into the realm of absolutely open nothingness, and transcends the world. This is the state before birth, and is also the state of the endless. When the path leads back to the endless, body and mind are both sublimated and one merges in reality with the Tao. This is as much as a person can do.

The ignorant project the spirit by staring in mirrors, by silently concentrating on the top of the head, or by facing a wall and forgetting the body. This is wrong. The spirit liberated by the gold elixir is the celestial spirit, while the spirit projected by all the quietistic practices is the mundane spirit. The celestial spirit is eternal, unborn and unperishing; the mundane spirit, not having undergone refinement, is subject to reincarnation. Unless one attains the science of the gold elixir to transform it, even if one can project and recall the mundane spirit at will and can know the past and future, one cannot escape transmigration. This is referred to by the saying, "Even if you last thousands of aeons, in the end you will fall into utter destruction."

These last seven diagrams represent the process of producing immortals, reversing the usual natural process. The foregoing fourteen diagrams give a general idea of going along with creation and reversal of creation. Following this I will bring up essential symbolic terms, distinguish correct and erroneous interpretations, and give the true meanings, so that students may understand analogous terms.

The Gold Elixir

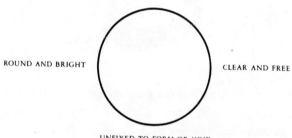

ROUND AND BRIGHT   CLEAR AND FREE

UNFIXED TO FORM OR VOID
INCLUDING TRUTHFULNESS AND ILLUMINATION

Gold is something stable and incorruptible; an elixir pill is something round, complete, luminous, pure, without defect. Ancient immortals used the term *gold elixir* as a metaphor of the essence of true consciousness, which is fundamentally complete and illumined.

In Confucianism, this essence is called the universal ultimate; in Buddhism, it is called complete awareness; in Taoism, it is called the gold elixir. Though there are three names, the reality is one. Confucians who cultivate this become sages; Buddhists who cultivate this become buddhas; Taoists who cultivate this become immortals. The adepts of all three teachings consider the fundamental true essence to be the basis of attainment of the Way.

The ignorant who do not know this consider the gold elixir to be a potion made from minerals. This is wrong. The true essence is matured through firing in the furnace of Creation, and lasts as long as heaven and earth, having the same light as sun and moon; how can it be made by mundane material substances?

The Heart of Heaven and Earth

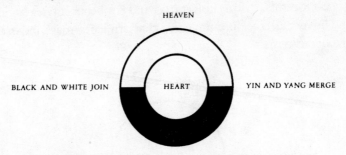

HEAVEN

BLACK AND WHITE JOIN   HEART   YIN AND YANG MERGE

TRANQUIL, UNPERTURBED   EARTH   SENSITIVE, EFFECTIVE

The first essential step in cultivating reality is to find the heart of heaven and earth. The heart of heaven and earth, the universal mind, is what has been previously referred to as the natural, innocent true mind. This mind is subtle and recondite, and is not easily manifested; it only shows a glimpse when "light appears in the empty room" and "within darkness, suddenly there is illumination."

Heaven is associated with yang, earth is associated with yin; the heart of heaven and earth is the mind in which yin is not separate from yang, yang is not separate from yin, yin and yang are merged. When yin and yang are conjoined, this mind is present; when yin and yang separate, this mind is absent. It is not form, not void, yet both form and void; it is not being, not nonbeing, yet both being and nonbeing. Form and void interpenetrate, being and nonbeing cannot be established; this is ineffable existence within true emptiness. When you know this mind and keep it intact, the overall basis is already established and the rest is easy.

On the Firing Process

The ignorant who do not know this all manipulate the avaricious physical heart; some consider the active mind the heart of heaven and earth, some consider the still mind the heart of heaven and earth, some think the mind dwelling on the middle of the torso is the heart of heaven and earth. This is all wrong. The avaricious heart is the conditioned human mind with personal desires; the active mind clings to existence, the still mind clings to nothingness, the dwelling mind fixes on form. These minds are as far from the heart of heaven and earth as mud is from the clouds.

The heart of heaven and earth is unified in action and stillness, is tranquil and unperturbed yet sensitive and effective, is sensitive and effective yet tranquil and unperturbed. How could it refer to the physical, avaricious heart?

The Crescent Moon Furnace

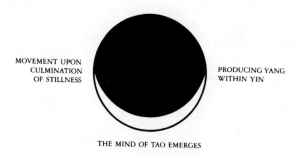

MOVEMENT UPON CULMINATION OF STILLNESS

PRODUCING YANG WITHIN YIN

THE MIND OF TAO EMERGES

The crescent moon is the moon in the beginning of its phase, beginning to shine again after having become totally dark; this symbolizes the sudden manifestation of the celestial root in people when they have attained utter stillness. This celestial root is called the mind of Tao. A furnace is a vessel in which fire is used; because the mind of Tao has a celestial light which can be used to burn away a person's mundanity, the mind of Tao is also represented as a furnace. Actually, the mind of Tao is the heart of heaven and earth; in terms of substance it is called the heart of heaven and earth; in terms of function it is called the mind of Tao. The two names refer to the same thing.

The ignorant who do not know this observe the crescent shape of the Chinese character for *heart* and erroneously consider the physical heart to be the crescent moon furnace. Also, those who practice sexual yoga consider the vulva to be the crescent moon furnace. These interpretations are both wrong. The crescent moon furnace is the light of the mind of Tao shining; where this light shines, all falsehood vanishes and one can become a sage and an immortal.

Tz'u-yang said, "Stop wasting your time by an alchemical stove; to refine the elixir you must seek the crescent moon furnace." He also said, "In the crescent moon furnace, jade flowers grow; in the cinnabar crucible, mercury is level. After harmonious blending by the power of fire, the seeds have yellow sprouts which gradually grow and develop." By this we can know the meaning of the crescent moon furnace.

The Cinnabar Crucible

UTTERLY EMPTY
UTTERLY ETHEREAL

SPIRIT

SENSITIVE
RESPONSIVE

THE ORIGINAL SPIRIT IS EVER-PRESENT
DISCRIMINATION DOES NOT ARISE

Cinnabar is the color of fire. Because fire can refine things, getting rid of old encrustation and restoring them like new, the phenomenon of fire, represented by a cinnabar crucible, most efficacious, most miraculous, able to transmute things, symbolizes the spiritual illumination in people, which shines everywhere and accomplishes everything.

But there is the original spirit, and then there is the discriminating spirit. The discriminating spirit can frustrate the Tao, the original spirit can attain the Tao. Because of the encrustation of the faculties of the discriminating spirit through its history, it uses the awareness of the original spirit to create illusions, never stopping until the loss of essence and life.

Practice of the universal science requires using the original spirit to control the discriminating spirit. When the discriminating spirit does not arise, aberrant fire goes out; when aberrant fire goes out, true fire arises. When true fire arises, the harmonious energy is fertile and the mechanism of life does not cease; so there is hope of attaining the universal Tao.

The ignorant who do not know this mistake the conscious discriminating spirit for the original spirit. This is wrong. The original spirit is the nonpsychic spirit, its consciousness most real, its reality most conscious. The conscious discriminating spirit is the psychic spirit; though conscious, there is artificiality in it. Conciousness in the midst of artificiality is the seed of compulsive habit and routine. An ancient adept said, "The root of infinite ages of birth and death, the ignorant call the original being." The root of birth and death is this discriminating spirit.

The Opening of the Mysterious Female

THE DOOR OF
YIN AND YANG

THE GATE OF
ACTION AND STILLNESS

THE PLACE UNTOUCHED BY THE PHYSICAL ELEMENTS

Mysterious stands for yang, for strength, for action; *female* stands for yin, for flexibility, for stillness. The opening of the mysterious female is the aperture of yin and yang, the door of strength and flexibility, the gate of action and stillness; it has no direction, no location, no shape, no form. It is like an opening hung in space, where the five elements cannot reach, where the physical elements cannot touch. Ultimate nonbeing, it contains ultimate being; ultimate emptiness, it contains ultimate fulfillment. This is the opening within the conjunction of yin and yang.

The ignorant who do not know this take mouth and nose to be the mysterious female. This is wrong. The mouth and nose are the gate through which the breath exits and enters, not the gate through which yin and yang enter. When yin and yang conjoin, they produce immortals and buddhas; can the air breathed in and out produce immortals and buddhas? *Understanding Reality* says, "Few are they who know the opening of the mysterious female; do not act at random with the nose and mouth."

The Opening of the Mysterious Pass

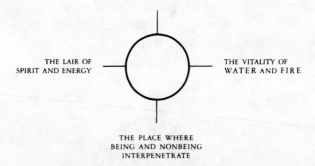

THE LAIR OF
SPIRIT AND ENERGY

THE VITALITY OF
WATER AND FIRE

THE PLACE WHERE
BEING AND NONBEING
INTERPENETRATE

The mysterious pass is a most recondite and abstruse passageway. It is also called the door of life and death, the chamber of vivifying and killing, the border of divinity and humanity, the gate of punishment and reward, the opening of being and nonbeing, the lair of spirit and energy, the ground of emptiness and fulfillment, the crossroads, and many other names. All of these terms depict this one opening. The mysterious pass is another name for the mysterious female. Because its recondite subtlety is unfathomable, it is called the mysterious pass; because yin and yang are herein, it is called the mysterious female. Really it is just this one opening.

The ignorant who do not know this sometimes take the space below the heart and above the genitals to be the mysterious pass; some consider the center of the umbilical region to be the mysterious pass; some call the coccyx the mysterious pass; some take the center of the spine, where it joins the ribs, to be the mysterious pass. These are all wrong. The mysterious pass has no fixed position; if it had a fixed position, it would not be the mysterious pass.

Ch'en Hsu-pai referred to the point where thought arises as the mysterious pass; this seems to be correct, but really is not. The point where thought arises already has fallen into the realm of temporal form; how can it be considered the mysterious pass?

I now clearly point out to you that the mysterious pass lies in subtle abstraction, where being and nonbeing interpenetrate. *Understanding Reality* says, "Seek the image of being in the subtle; seek the true vitality in the recondite. From this being and nonbeing interpenetrate; before you have seen it, how can you imagine it?" Also, the *Four Hundred Words on the Gold Elixir* says, "This opening is not an ordinary aperture; made by HEAVEN and EARTH together, it is called the lair of spirit and energy. Within are the vitalities of WATER and FIRE." These passages truly point out the opening of the mysterious pass.

The Valley Spirit

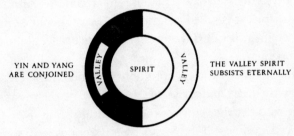

YIN AND YANG ARE CONJOINED   VALLEY   SPIRIT   VALLEY   THE VALLEY SPIRIT SUBSISTS ETERNALLY

THE VALLEY IS FILLED WITH UNITY

The valley spirit is the spirit of open valleys. Between two high mountains is a valley; when people shout into it, the valley conveys their voices, so it is called the valley spirit. In Taoist practice this is used to symbolize the spirit of open awareness in people. This is because when the mind is open it is effectively aware; if it is not open, it is not effectively aware. The effective awareness comes from openness; this is called the valley spirit.

Spiritual means formless, imageless, ethereal, unfathomable. This spirit is that which is "tranquil and unperturbed, sensitive and effective." The so-called solidification of the spiritual embryo is also this spirit.

The ignorant who do not know this think that the valley spirit means the spirit focused on the "valley of heaven" (at the top of the head); some call concentration of the spirit in the "yellow court" (in the middle of the torso) nurturing the valley spirit. This is wrong. If you say the spirit focuses on the valley of heaven or concentrates in the yellow court, then it is not open; without openness, how can there be spirit? Not open, no spirit—how can it be called the valley spirit?

Understanding Reality says, "If you want to attain the eternal immortality of the valley spirit, you must set up the foundation on the mysterious female. When true vitality has returned to the golden room, a pearl of spiritual light never leaves." The mysterious female is integrated and open within; being open, true awareness is ever-present and does not become obscure. True vitality, spiritual light, and the valley spirit, all symbolize true awareness.

The Gold Crucible and the Jade Furnace

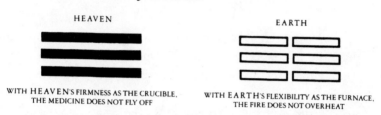

HEAVEN

EARTH

WITH HEAVEN'S FIRMNESS AS THE CRUCIBLE, THE MEDICINE DOES NOT FLY OFF

WITH EARTH'S FLEXIBILITY AS THE FURNACE, THE FIRE DOES NOT OVERHEAT

The gold crucible is something firm, strong, stable; this symbolizes single-minded concentration of will, by which one can bear the Tao. The jade furnace is something warm, flexible, even, peaceful; it symbolizes gradual progress of the work, by which one can persevere long and go far. The gold crucible is also called the crucible of HEAVEN; the jade furnace is also called the furnace of EARTH.

Ignorant people who do not know this cast iron crucibles, build clay stoves, and fire metals and minerals, vainly imagining that they will form the elixir in this way. This is wrong. This is because material furnaces and crucibles can only refine material medicines used for ordinary purposes; they cannot refine the immaterial elixir of immortality.

An ancient immortal said, "The crucible basically is no crucible, and the furnace is not a furnace either." What the furnace and crucible refer to is the fact that practice of the Tao can only be accomplished when firmness and flexibility are both employed. This is like a chemist needing a furnace for the crucible and needing a crucible for the furnace; only when equipped with both furnace and crucible can one make medicine.

The Medicinal Substances of Raven and Rabbit

WATER—MOON   FIRE—SUN

HAVING CHASED THE TWO THINGS BACK INTO THE YELLOW PATH,
HOW CAN THE GOLD ELIXIR FAIL TO DEVELOP?

There is a golden raven in the sun, which is the yin within yang; there is a jade rabbit in the moon, which is the yang within yin. Among the trigrams, the sun is FIRE ☲ , yang outside and yin inside, symbolizing the presence of flexibility within strength. Among the trigrams, the moon is WATER ☵ , yin outside and yang inside, symbolizing the presence of strength within flexibility. The science of spiritual alchemy is simply a matter of taking flexibility within strength and strength within flexibility, which are the two great medicines of true yin and true yang, and fusing them into one energy, thus forming the elixir. The reason that true yin and true yang are called medicines is that it is possible thereby to accomplish rejuvenation and extension of life. The so-called intertwining of tortoise and snake, and the mutual settling of water and fire, both represent this principle; it is just a matter of picking convenient images to represent the path of unification of true yin and true yang.

The ignorant who do not know this are confused by the words *raven* and *rabbit*, which conventionally stand for sun and moon; some practice the "inhalation" of sunlight and moonlight into the mouth; some practice taking in sunlight and moonlight with the eyes. This is wrong. In the sky there are the sun and moon of the sky; in humans there are the sun and moon of humans. The true yin and true yang of the human being are the raven and rabbit, sun and moon, of humans. The sun and moon in the sky are far away from us—how can their light be collected? Even supposing something is collected, it is external energy that can cause harm; if you do these practices of taking light into the mouth and eyes for a long time, they will result in swelling and blindness. So there is no benefit, but rather harm.

Dragon and Tiger Meet

LAKE—METAL   THUNDER—WOOD

THE DRAGON COMES FROM THE EASTERN SEA.
THE TIGER APPEARS IN THE WESTERN MOUNTAINS.
THE TWO BEASTS HAVE A BATTLE
AND TURN INTO THE MARROW OF HEAVEN AND EARTH.

The nature of the dragon is flexible; it enlivens beings. Associated with wood, among the trigrams it corresponds to THUNDER ☳ . This symbolizes the flexible essence of human beings. THUNDER, though basically yang, is taken as a symbol of flexibility because there is less yang than yin. The nature of the tiger is strong; it kills beings. Associated with metal, among the trigrams it corresponds to LAKE ☱ . This symbolizes firm sense in human beings. LAKE, though basically yin, is taken as a symbol of strength because there is more yang than yin.

When this essence and this sense are separated, they become temperament and emotion, resulting in injury. When they are conjoined they are true essence and true sense, enhancing life. The meeting of dragon and tiger is seeking sense through essence and returning sense to essence, meaning that essence and sense unite. Images such as the maid of the eastern house and the man of the western house joining in matrimony, the eldest son and the youngest daughter uniting, and metal and wood combining, all symbolize this merging of true essence and true sense.

The ignorant who do not know this consider the liver as the dragon and the lungs as the tiger, and say that the mating of the dragon and tiger means circulating the energies of liver and lungs in the umbilical center, in the lower abdomen, or in the middle of the torso. This is wrong. What they do not realize is that the energies of liver and lungs are conditioned physical energies; not only can they not be joined into one, but their forced aggregation will, if continued for a long time, produce an ailment that cannot be cured, hastening one's death. Is that not foolish?

Inversion of FIRE *and* WATER

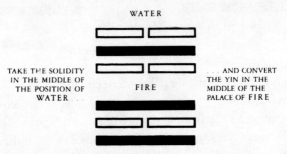

FIRE AND WATER SETTLE EACH OTHER

The trigram WATER ☵ is yin outside and yang inside; the trigram FIRE ☲ is yang outside and yin inside. Inner yang constitutes water; outer yang makes fire. The science of alchemy takes the yang in WATER and fills in the yin in FIRE, using water to settle fire. This is called water rising and fire descending, water and fire being inverted. This symbolizes the spiritual water of real knowledge of the mind of Tao controlling the aberrant fire of conscious knowledge of the human mind.

Our real knowledge is dark outside and light inside, like WATER ☵ being yin outside and yang inside. Our conscious knowledge is light outside and dark inside, like FIRE ☲ being yang outside and yin inside. Controlling conscious knowledge by real knowledge, submitting to real knowledge by conscious knowledge, reality and consciousness are unified and crystallize into the elixir. This is likened to inverting WATER and FIRE so that water and fire settle each other. Such images as the boy and girl, the black lead and red mercury, also depict the uniting of real knowledge and conscious knowledge.

The ignorant who do not know this say the genitals are WATER and the heart is FIRE, and consider inversion of WATER and FIRE to mean conveying the energy of the genitals upward to combine with the heart, while the energy of the heart descends to the genitals. There are also those who gather the bedroom elixir, taking the boy and girl to actually mean a man and a woman, considering the inversion of WATER and FIRE to mean sexual intercourse with the man below and the woman above. Also, chemists take the inversion of WATER and FIRE to mean using lead to stabilize mercury, or to refer to building a fire in the furnace below while keeping water in the crucible above. These are all wrong. The part of cultivating reality is a matter of working on the reality; all aberrant practices and abominations dealing with form and polluted material substance are artificial, not real—how can one attain reality thereby?

Reversal of the Five Elements

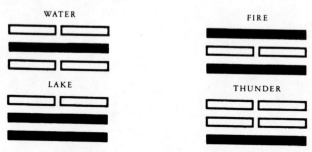

WHEN THE FIVE ELEMENTS DO NOT GO IN ORDER,
THE DRAGON EMERGES FROM THE FIRE;
WITH THE ART OF REVERSING THE FIVE ELEMENTS,
THE TIGER EMERGES IN THE WATER.

When the five elements go in order, wood produces fire, metal produces water; when the five elements are reversed, fire produces wood, water produces metal. The wood produced by fire is wood that never decays, like wood that is treated by fire to become charcoal and lasts forever in the ground. The metal produced by water is metal that never rusts, like gold in a smelting furnace liquefying, then forming an ingot with uncommon brilliance.

Fire producing wood symbolizes the fundamental essence of human beings refined in the furnace of evolution to become permanently stable essence. Water producing metal symbolizes the true sense in human beings crossing over the waves of the ocean of desire to become permanently undefiled sense. This is what is meant by the saying of the ancient immortals, "When the five elements go in order, the universe is a pit of fire; when the five elements are reversed, the whole world is made of jewels."

The ignorant who do not know this consider mental circulation of energy horizontally and vertically within the body to be the reversal of the five elements. This is wrong. What they do not realize is that the body is wholly mundane; the internal organs and external faculties are all temporary things, becoming a pile of stinking bones and flesh when respiration stops—where is there anything real? It is an impossible dream to be able to comprehend essence and life through these temporary things.

The Yellow Woman Go-Between

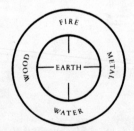

IF FIRE AND WATER DO NOT HAVE EARTH,
EVEN IF THEY INCLUDE THE FOUR FORMS,
THEY CANNOT FORM THE ELIXIR.

The "yellow woman" is the earth mother in the center, called the yellow woman because it can harmonize yin and yang and can combine the four forms. The alchemical treatises use this to symbolize the true faith within the true intent in people, which can harmonize essence and sense, and nurture vitality and energy. True intent and true faith are the yellow woman in our being; this is what is referred to as the central communicative principle.

Ignorant people who do not know this think the yellow woman go-between means mentally conveying the energies of the internal organs so that they conjoin. Then there are also mischief-makers who use glib procuresses to encourage sexual encounters so that they can take the first sexual fluids of virgins, and call this the yellow woman acting as go-between. This is wrong. The true earth has no position, true intent has no form; producing all things, containing all principles, it is possible thereby to join vitality, energy, and spirit, and to assemble the five elements—that is why it is called the yellow woman go-between. This term does not refer to mental gymnastics or to procuresses.

The Twin Poles of the Two Eights

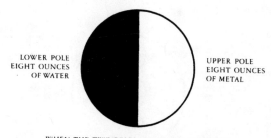

LOWER POLE
EIGHT OUNCES
OF WATER

UPPER POLE
EIGHT OUNCES
OF METAL

WHEN THE TWO POLES JOIN THEIR VITALITIES,
THE BODY OF HEAVEN AND EARTH FORMS

From the time of the new moon, the moon communicates with the sun; on the third day of the lunar month, a slight light appears. Then on the eighth, the yang within yin is at the halfway point, like a strung bow; this is called the upper pole. On the sixteenth, the slight darkness of one yin appears on the full moon. Then on the twenty-third, the yin within yang is at the halfway point, again like a strung bow; this is called the lower pole.

At the upper pole is obtained eight ounces of the metal within water; at the lower pole is obtained eight ounces of the water within metal: the two eights making one pound, metal and water stabilizing each other, is a symbol of yin and yang joining. Alchemical texts use this to allude to the balance of strength and flexibility, without partiality, without bias, perfectly centered, correctly aligned.

Ignorant people who do not know this sometimes think a male reaching the age of sixteen is the full complement of the energies of the twin poles of the two eights, and then they stop emission of semen. Others take the two eights to mean eight ounces of lead and eight ounces of mercury, and cook these into a potion to ingest. Both are wrong. The two poles are yin and yang. The firm strength of HEAVEN ☰ is yang, and the yielding flexibility of EARTH ☷ is yin. When yin and yang mate, the body of HEAVEN and EARTH is formed, and the basis of the elixir forms. This is the meaning of the twin poles.

The Tiny Pearl

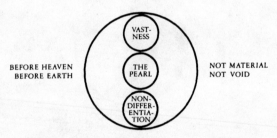

THE UNIVERSAL ONE CONTAINS THE TRUE ENERGY

Before people are born, when they are in the womb, there is an undifferentiated darkness; they are just in a swirl of unified energy, with nothing else. This is what is called the universal One containing the true energy. This energy is utterly spiritual, utterly ineffable, utterly open, utterly miraculous; it is ultimate nonbeing, yet contains ultimate being. The three bases, eight trigrams, four forms, and five elements, are all contained therein; so though it is formless, it can produce manifestations, which are endless—the organs and members of the body all develop naturally from it. Because it is utterly spiritual, utterly ineffable, utterly open, and utterly miraculous, it is also called true awareness, and it is also called the nonpsychological spirit.

In the womb, one energy containing reality is called the real energy; after leaving the womb, awareness containing the one energy is called conscious energy. One energy is the substance; this is real emptiness. True awareness is the function; this is ineffable existence. True energy, true awareness, real emptiness, ineffable existence—though the names are different, it is just one reality. This reality is formless, imperceptible, indescribable; it is so subtle that the ancient immortals called this reality a tiny pearl. Yet though they call it a tiny pearl, in reality it has no such shape; they call it thus because there is a point of conscious energy hidden in the center, and because that point of awareness contains the whole cosmos, space, and the universe. In reality it is the original energy which is prior to the bifurcation of the vast nondifferentiation of primal unity.

Ignorant people who do not know this take a blood clot of a girl's first menses to be the tiny pearl. Also, yogins take the tiny pearl to mean the outpouring of the light of the eyes after long concentration of the mind on the "hall of illumination," the spot one inch inside the point between the eyebrows. Both of these are wrong. The tiny pearl of primordial nondifferentiation is the jewel of consciousness which can produce saints and sages, immortals and buddhas—how could it be made by blood, or by the light of visualization?

The *Four Hundred Words on the Gold Elixir* says, "Primal unity contains space, space contains the universe; when you find the root source, it is the size of a tiny grain." San-feng said, "Who does not know, who does not understand, who does not act—all have gotten lost on the bead of primal nondifferentiation."

The Hexagram Signs of the Firing Process

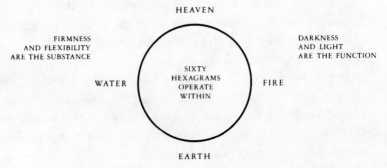

THE YANG FIRE HAS ITS TIME; THE YIN CONVERGENCE HAS ITS PERIOD.

The alchemical classics use the sixty-four hexagrams to represent the principles of the yang fire and the yin convergence. The two hexagrams HEAVEN ☰☰ and EARTH ☷☷ are taken for the crucible and furnace because the firmness of yang and the flexibility of yin are considered the substance. The two hexagrams WATER ☵☵ and FIRE ☲☲ are taken for the medicinal substances because the balance of firmness and flexibility is considered the function.

The two hexagrams RETURN ☷☳ and MEETING ☰☴ are the borders of intercourse of yin and yang; they are taken to illustrate that the use of firmness and the use of flexibility each have their time. The two hexagrams DIFFICULTY ☵☳ and DARKNESS ☶☵ are the beginning of evolution; they are taken to represent the necessity of using firmness when the fire is to be advanced and the necessity of using flexibility when the fire is to be withdrawn. SETTLED ☵☲ and UNSETTLED ☲☵ are the end of evolution; they are taken to represent how the use of firmness with the yang fire should not be excessive and the use of flexibility with the yin convergence should not be insufficient.

The remaining fifty-four hexagrams all follow HEAVEN, EARTH, WATER, FIRE, RETURN, MEETING, DIFFICULTY, DARKNESS, SETTLED, and UNSETTLED in their application, naturally being so. It is all a matter of the balancing and unification of yin and yang.

The ignorant who do not know this apply the sixty-four hexagrams to the terrestrial time of calendar and clock and perform forced practices on this framework. This is wrong. The creative energy of yin and yang of heaven and earth flows in cycles, without beginning or end, not according to the sequence of sixty-four hexagrams. The sixty-four hexagrams were made by a sage who observed heaven and earth and understood the evolution of yin and yang; the sixty-four hexagrams are just explanatory notes on the evolution of yin and yang. When the evolution of the human being and the evolution of heaven and earth are in concert, there are naturally the sixty-four hexagrams—one should not get mired in the words and cling to the symbols.

The Gate of Birth of the Self

THE MEDICINE COMES
FROM THE SOUTHWEST,
THE POSITION OF EARTH

IF YOU WANT TO SEEK
THE POSITION OF EARTH,
IS IT APART FROM
THE HUMAN BEING?

GAINING A COMPANION
IN THE SOUTHWEST

When the moon reaches the southwest, darkness culminates and light is born. The southwest is associated with EARTH, which is pure yin. The arising of one yang at the bottom of pure yin has the form of EARTH ☷ above and THUNDER ☳ below, making the hexagram RETURN. In terms of the phases of the moon, this is the upturned crescent. These images both symbolize the sudden appearance of the celestial mind in the midst of extreme quiet. This is also called the mind of Tao and the natural, innocent true mind; it is what was referred to before as the crescent moon furnace.

If you see this mind, preserve it intact, and use it to promote the celestial and withdraw the mundane, with the sustained attention of a cat waiting to pounce on a mouse, you will naturally reach the point where the celestial gradually grows and the mundane gradually recedes. When mundanity is exhausted and the celestial is pure, one is an immortal. Therefore the southwest position of EARTH is called the gate of birth of the self, or the gate of giving life to the self.

The ignorant who do not know this think the gate of birth of the self is the female birth canal. This is wrong. The birth canal gives birth to humans—how can it give birth to immortals?

The Door of Killing the Self

CELESTIAL ENERGY
NEARLY EXHAUSTED

MUNDANE ENERGY
NEARLY TOTAL

LOSING COMPANIONSHIP
IN THE NORTHEAST

From the northeast, the yang light of the moon is about to disappear. The northeast is associated with MOUNTAIN ☶ , in which the yin energy is about to become total and the yang light is very slight. This stage is represented by the hexagram STRIPPING AWAY, which has MOUNTAIN ☶ above and EARTH ☷ below; in terms of the phases of the moon, this is the overturned bowl. These both symbolize external influences, acquired energies, stripping away the real, the original. Those of great power who suddenly awaken and turn around use this bit of remaining yang to break through darkness with light, applying effort to cultivate and sustain it; then it is not hard to return to the fundamental and restore the original.

On the Firing Process

Ordinary people who are deluded and unawakened go along with the force of mundanity as it strips away the celestial; then when the celestial is exhausted and the mundane is total, it is impossible not to die. The *I ching* calls this "losing companionship in the northeast." Alchemical texts also call it the door of killing the self.

The ignorant who do not know this think the birth canal of the female is the door of killing the self. This is wrong. The gate of birth and the door of death are both immaterial, formless passageways. By following mundanity one dies, by returning the celestial one lives; hence the names *gate of birth* and *door of killing*. In reality, they are just one opening. When ancient immortals called this the pass of life and death, though they called it a pass, again this was just a matter of terminology—it has no location, no place.

Understanding Reality says, "Make the door of death the door of life; do not call the gate of life the gate of death. If you understand the killing mechanism and know how to reverse it, for the first time you will realize there is giving life within killing." Based on this, we can know the meaning of the gate of birth and the door of killing.

The Opening of Doing

CINNABAR/RED DRAGON

FIRE

METAL VITALITY
WHITE TIGER

METAL

WOOD

WOOD MERCURY
BLUE DRAGON

WATER

SPIN YIN AND YANG.

TAKE OVER EVOLUTION.

WITH DESIRE, WATCH THE OPENING.

The path of doing is the work of "watching the opening with desire." Watching the opening means watching the opening of the evolution of yin and yang. The course of work, the orderly procedure—using the temporal to restore the primordial, combining the four forms, assembling the five elements, gathering the medicines, operating the fire, from restoring the elixir to forming the embryo—is all within that opening. Without the verbal communication and mental transmission of a true teacher, a slight miss causes a great loss.

The ignorant who do not know this take the path of doing to be manipulation of circulation in the temporal unreal physical body. This is wrong. The science of the gold elixir is the study of the primordial, whereby it is possible to spin yin and yang, take over evolution, reverse the mechanism of energy, invert heaven and earth, and be in primordial accord with nature. It cannot be accomplished by manipulation of the conditioned physical body.

Cheng-yang said, "Tears, saliva, gastric fluid, semen, air, blood, and lymph, the seven marvelous substances, are all mundane—if you take these things as the basis of the elixir, how can you fly aloft to the celestial realms?" Tz'u-yang said, "Saliva, semen, and breath are humanly manipulated. Only when you have elixir can you evolve. If there is no true seed in the crucible, it is like cooking with an empty pot." The adepts are those who recognize the real— the path of doing is not easy to know.

The Subtlety of Nondoing

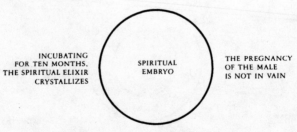

The path of nondoing is the work of watching the subtlety without desire, and takes place after the formation of the spiritual embryo. This is calmly watching the subtlety of the development of the unified energy. After the spiritual embryo has formed, the temporal has been returned to the primordial; then one just uses the work of bathing and incubating, without either neglect or obsession, operating the natural real fire to bring about the transmutation by which the formless spontaneously produces form and the immaterial produces substance. When fully developed, the infant emerges, like a ripe melon falling from the vine; then the intense effort that had been hitherto applied is abandoned and no longer applied.

The ignorant who do not know this, without having found out what essence and life are and what practice of the Tao is, learn some auxiliary methods, roundabout routes, minor techniques, and immediately go into the mountains to practice quiet sitting, or shut off their senses and still their minds, and consider this to be nondoing. This is wrong.

Essence and life must be cultivated as a pair; the work requires two phases. The first of these two phases is doing, by which one comprehends life; next comes nondoing, by which one comprehends essence. How can one comprehend essence and life by empty, quiet sitting and stilling the mind?

Understanding Reality says, "Before you have refined the restored elixir, do not go into the mountains; in the mountains, nothing within or without is real knowledge. This ultimate treasure is in everyone—it is just that the ignorant do not fully recognize it." It also says, "Beginning with doing, no one sees; when nondoing is reached, everyone knows. Only seeing nondoing as the essential marvel, do you not realize that doing is the foundation?" By this we can know that doing and nondoing each have their time, each have their function; they are very dissimilar.

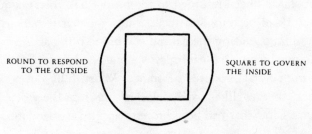

ROUND TO RESPOND
TO THE OUTSIDE

SQUARE TO GOVERN
THE INSIDE

MERGING WITH THE ORDINARY WORLD, PEOPLE DO NOT KNOW YOU;
HARMONIZING ILLUMINATION, THE TAO IS EASY TO COMPLETE.

Merging with the ordinary world and harmonizing illumination is the function of the great hermit who is concealed in the city. Merging with the ordinary world means mixing with the people without letting them know of one's real inner state; harmonizing illumination means harmonization without imitation, being in the world yet transcending the world. When able to mix with the ordinary world and harmonize enlightenment, one is outwardly round and able to respond to people, while inwardly square and autonomous. Using the phenomena of the world to practice the principles of the Tao, one may appear or disappear, rebel or conform, without hindrance; then practice of the Tao is very easy.

The ignorant who do not know this sometimes imagine that merging with the ordinary world and harmonizing illumination means dealing with affairs in the daytime and practicing quietude at night. This is wrong. This might be called following the ordinary world, but not merging with the world; it may be called concealing illumination, but not harmonizing illumination.

Merging with the ordinary world and harmonizing illumination has the power to take over the evolution of heaven and earth; it is the secret whereby one can appropriate the vivifying and killing of yin and yang. It is not easy to know, and not easy to do.

On the Firing Process

The Medicine Goes Back in the Earth Pot

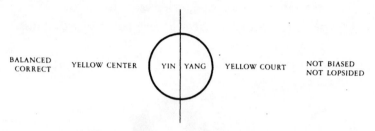

VITALITY, ENERGY, AND SPIRIT MERGE INTO ONE ENERGY.

The nature of earth is warm and soft; thus it can nurture beings. Cooking in a pot can complete things. Therefore a pot referred to as earth means a vessel which nurtures and completes. This is not ordinary earth, not an ordinary pot. The medicine going back in the earth pot is a symbol for the work of incubation, gentle nurturance, of the spiritual embryo formed by the joining of yin and yang.

Incubation of the spiritual embryo is all a matter of single-minded attention not scattering, persistently keeping to the center, yin and yang not being imbalanced. Therefore it is called the earth pot, since earth symbolizes the center; when you get down to the reality, it simply means central balance. If you keep to the center, yin and yang combine, the five elements assemble, and the spiritual embryo becomes complete. If you lose the center, yin and yang become lopsided, imbalanced, the five elements disintegrate, and the spirital embryo is damaged. So keeping to the center, maintaining balance, is the secret of nurturing the spiritual embryo.

The ignorant who do not know this sometimes dig out earth ovens, heat up cinnabar, and take quicksilver from cinnabar, calling the earth oven the earth pot. Others melt lead in a clay oven with a reservoir of ash, and call the reservoir of ash the earth pot. They are all wrong.

Tzu-yeh said, "The true earth has no position, true intent has no form." It is because the "earth pot" which is the center has no form, no appearance, no location, no place, that it can develop and complete the spiritual embryo. It does not mean a clay vessel.

Solidifying the Spiritual Embryo

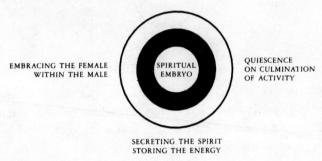

EMBRACING THE FEMALE WITHIN THE MALE

SPIRITUAL EMBRYO

QUIESCENCE ON CULMINATION OF ACTIVITY

SECRETING THE SPIRIT STORING THE ENERGY

The spiritual embryo is the embryonic sage, the fundamental state of the infant, without discrimination or knowledge. When you reach the state of absence of discrimination or knowledge, the spirit is unified, objects disappear, and you enter into a state of profound trance without differentiation, entering from doing into nondoing.

Ignorant people who do not know this think that conveying the energies of heart and genitals to mix in the solar plexus region is the spiritual embryo; some consider concentration of the mind in the midtorso to be the spiritual embryo; some say the spiritual embryo means conveying energy up the spine and down the front of the body, finally dwelling in the lower abdomen. All of these are wrong. The spiritual embryo is formless and immaterial; though it is called an embryo, in reality there is no embryo to be seen. The term *embryo* just describes true awareness becoming solidified, stabilized, not scattering. If you forcibly coagulate a corpuscle of air and blood, that is a ghost embryo which hastens death, not the spiritual embryo of eternal life.

On the Firing Process

In Ten Months the Embryo Is Complete

SPIRIT COMPLETE
ENERGY REPLETE

MUNDANITY EXHAUSTED
THE CELESTIAL PURE

THE GREAT RESTORED ELIXIR OF GOLD LIQUID

The completeness of the embryo in ten months is a symbol of completeness of spirit, repleteness of energy, mental accretions gone, acquired influences dissolved, mundanity exhausted, the celestial pure. It is like pregnancy being completed in ten lunar months; but when it is said that the method of the gold elixir is completed in ten months, this is just using the metaphor of pregnancy—it means that after the spiritual embryo is solidified, it is necessary to ward off danger and gently nurture it until it is fully developed, without any lack; it does not mean there is a fixed period of ten months.

The ignorant who do not know this are misled by the words *ten months,* and actually take ten months as a fixed period, during which they practice energy circulation, visualization, or mental freezing, by which they imagine they will solidify the embryo. This is wrong. The path of cultivation of reality, from gathering the medicines, refining them, crystallizing the elixir, solidifying the embryo, to release and transmutation, requires boundless effort—how could it be limited to ten months? By this we can know that *ten months* is just a symbolic term.

The Infant Emerges

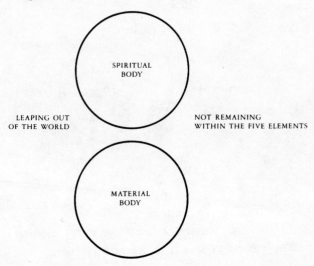

THERE IS A BODY OUTSIDE THE BODY.

The emergence of the infant means the release and transmutation of the spiritual embryo. The spiritual embryo means that within the material body there is also a spiritual body; release and transmutation mean that the spiritual body is born from the material body. Because a spiritual body is born from within the material body, this is likened to a woman giving birth after ten months of pregnancy, producing an infant. Therefore the spiritual body is called the infant. When the infant emerges, there is a body outside the body, leaping out of the world, not remaining within the five elements, avoiding transmigration, having the same life span as heaven and earth, the same age as sun and moon.

The ignorant who do not know this take the true yang within WATER ☵ to be the spiritual body, the infant; some take the vital energy in the genitals to be the spiritual-body infant. The infant within WATER is yang within yin; the spiritual-body infant is the reality of the merging and sublimation of yin and yang. As for the energy within the genitals, this is a wildfire in the genitals, and does not have the meaning of the infant at all. They should not be mixed up.

Understanding Reality says, "The infant is the unified true energy; in ten months the embryo is complete, entering the spiritual foundation." The *Four Hundred Words on the Gold Elixir* says, "When husband and wife have intercourse, clouds and rain form in the bedroom. In a year is born an infant, and everyone rides on a crane." By this we can know what the infant of the spiritual body means.

Shifting the Furnace, Changing the Crucible

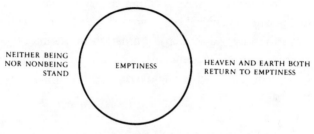

NEITHER BEING NOR NONBEING STAND — EMPTINESS — HEAVEN AND EARTH BOTH RETURN TO EMPTINESS

THE CRUCIBLE OF UNIVERSAL VOID
THE FURNACE OF NONDOING

When the great Tao is completely attained, there is a body outside the body, one is physically and mentally sublimated, and one has reached the stage of a great sage, there is no further need for furnace and crucible—why should there be such a thing as shifting the furnace, changing the crucible? The reason for shifting the furnace and changing the crucible is to store the spiritual body and secretly develop spiritual powers.

What is shifted is the furnace, what is changed is the crucible. Using universal void for the crucible and nondoing for the furnace, the former crucible of HEAVEN and the furnace of EARTH, the cinnabar crucible and the crescent moon furnace, as well as the medicinal substances, are no longer used. All that is used is the spiritual body. The spiritual body transmutes spontaneously in emptiness, becoming increasingly effective with increasing openness, becoming increasingly marvelous with increasing voidness. Its marvelous efficacy unfathomable, its transmutations endless, is what is called the child also producing grandchildren, and the grandchildren also branching out. Getting to this state, ceasing effort, breaking through space, and leaping up to the supreme infinite celestial realm—this is the perfect attainment.

Students of later times who have not gotten the authentic tradition sometimes suppose that having a body outside the body is the consummation of the Tao. This is not so. *The Song of Tapping the Lines* says, "When not a single thing exists, that finally reveals the Tao; in the five directions comes through the countenance of the real person. Immortal boys and girls greet one on colored clouds, and in the five palaces of illumination, pronouncements of truth are transmitted." Seeing this, we know that the ultimate accomplishment is only when the spiritual body can transmute in countless ways.

Part Three

Related Texts

FIFTY VERSES TO RESOLVE DOUBTS

1. *Detachment from the World*

Of worldly things, a thousandfold, not one is real;
The sentiments of mundane ties are most injurious to the being.
Cutting through with one stroke, there is nothing to bind you;
In the realm of liberation you become an independent person.

2. *Cultivation and Sleep*

Cutting down on sleep is really not removing the demon of sleep;
Forgetting to eat, neglecting to sleep, you cut through
    entanglements.
When entanglements are swept away and the mind is clear
    and calm,
You may sleep throughout the day and night—what is there
    to fear?

3. *Practice*

Practice developing virtue is the greatest priority;
When achievement is great and practice profound, it moves
    heaven and earth.
Ridiculous are the foolish ones who only profit themselves;
With no achievement and little action, they dream of becoming
    immortals.

4. *The Gold Elixir*

The primordial basic essence is called the elixir;
In the furnace of the eight trigrams it is forged into a pill.
The deluded throughout the world vainly seek external
   medicines;
By taking these, they wrongly imagine they can ascend to the
   clouds.

5. *The Mysterious Pass*

Few people know the opening of the mysterious pass;
Extremely subtle and recondite, it contains yin and yang.
Going along, you flow back into the road of affliction;
Coming back in reverse, this is the foundation of sages.

6. *The Discriminating Spirit*

The consciousness which thinks is called the discriminating
   spirit;
The seed of transmigration, it carries the accretions of the senses.
The ignorant and deluded both play with the wandering soul;
After all, who can see the host behind it all?

7. *The Celestial Vitality*

A point of celestial vitality is hidden in the physical being;
When you recognize the real, you can set your sights upon it.
It is not in the heart and not in the genitals;
Not void, not form, it is concealed in the mysterious pass.

8. *Primordial Energy*

The primordial unified energy is in the vast undifferentiated;
It has no shape or form, yet does not fall into voidness.
When you recognize the true state of the beginning of life,
Only then will you know there is a host within your self.

9. *The Primordial and the Conditioned*

Before birth is called the primordial;
Temperament comes along with emergence in the world.

The sages of yore and people of late are divided on two roads;
You should carefully distinguish the partial and complete.

10. *The Beginning of the Course*

The beginning of the course is basically the primal treasure,
The subtle, recondite, true unified vitality.
It is something unadulterated, flawless, pure;
Do not misapply this term to menstrual blood.

11. *Three Medicines*

The medicines are of three kinds—vitality, energy, and spirit;
Whatever has form is not the original reality.
Utterly pure, open and aware, these medicines
Are refined into the indestructible spiritual body.

12. *Essence and Life*

Essence and life are basically divided into primordial and
    temporal;
When the living body falls to the ground, it determines partial
    and complete.
Temporal essence and life follow the turns of fate;
Get hold of the primordial and you wield the authority yourself.

13. *The Heart of Heaven and Earth*

The heart of heaven and earth—where is it stored?
Yin and yang stimulate it to manifest a sphere of light.
Refining it in the crucible of openness and nonbeing,
Forever and ever it never wanes away.

14. *The Mind of Tao and the Human Mind*

The human mind is like iron, the mind of Tao like gold;
One should assess them carefully in terms of subtlety and
    insecurity.
The spiritual capacity of transmutation has no high or low;
At the fountainhead, the living water distinguishes yang and yin.

15. *Before Birth*

In the state before birth, who knows?
When silent, passive, undifferentiated,
The four forms and five elements do not reach;
The unified energy has no male or female.

16. *At Birth*

The newborn state—what is it like?
The primordial and the temporal are one energy.
No discrimination, no knowledge, not a single stain—
The seed of buddhas and immortals, the lair of sages.

17. *The Other*

The other is not another person;
If you mistake it for another, you are already way off.
Your child has wandered off outside—
Give it a call; when it sees your face, it will follow its parent.

18. *Other and Self*

The classics speak of other and self to distinguish yin and yang;
This is the realm of purity, neither material nor void.
Those who practice deviant techniques of sexual alchemy
Destroy their natural innocence in the brothels.

19. *Associates*

Associates should be divided into inner and outer supports;
With two or three people as personal associates,
And outer associates likewise helping out,
Shed the dust of personal history.

20. *Patrons*

People seek patrons, hoping to accomplish their practices;
Buying crucibles, smelting lead, they madly grasp for the wind.
How can they understand that the celestial mechanism transcends
    things of the world?
Depending on the power of others, they stick to their ignorance.

21. *The Ninefold Crucible*

The number nine associated with HEAVEN is called pure yang;
The method of refining restored elixir in the ninefold crucible
Is interpreted by the deluded to refer to women as crucibles—
They will surely enter an inescapable impasse.

22. *Summoning and Absorbing*

There is a secret method of summoning and absorbing the
    primordial;
Beckoning fulfillment by emptiness, you see the emperor of
    the void:
In the clamor of form and sound, there is no obstruction;
Freely you spin the north star.

23. *Inversion*

What difficulty is there in inverting yin and yang?
You should exercise spiritual observation in quietude.
When the mind of Tao is not obscured, the human mind
    vanishes;
Right away you ascend directly to the peak experience.

24. *The Firing Process*

The work of operating the fire basically has no time;
Working by day, introspective by night, you kill the inner
    parasites.
Warding off danger, wary of peril, ever clear and calm,
In dealing with people you adjust without error.

25. *The Hexagram Images*

For the firing process, the classics speak of the *I ching* hexagrams;
But it is wrong to ponder the lines and cling to the images.
It is all a matter of needing to understand the principle of yin
    and yang;
Advance or withdraw according to the time, as is indicated.

26. *The Furnace and Crucible of Heaven and Earth*

The crucible of HEAVEN and furnace of EARTH are in one's
    own body;
Stop inquiring externally after their basis.
When firmness and flexibility have no separation,
They forge the primal unified energy, the real.

27. *The Crescent Moon Furnace*

You ask what the crescent moon furnace is—
Within black there is white, returning after darkness.
Clearly I point out the matrix of the restored elixir
To waken the people of the time—do you know or not?

28. *The Cinnabar Crucible*

Cultivation of reality depends on the cinnabar crucible;
It is not iron, not gold, not silver.
Recognizing the light of awareness, you take the fresh,
Replacing the old, you see original humanity.

29. *The Earth Pot*

The earth pot is not made of earth;
The proper state of central balance is its true name.
Wood, metal, water, and fire, all gather herein,
Cultivating a mystic pearl that shines through the night.

30. *The Dipper Handle*

By watching the dipper handle as it turns in the sky,
You will realize that the mechanism of life is elsewhere.
Turning it around to retrieve autonomy within,
Then in the midst of the fire a golden lotus will appear.

31. *The Two Poles*

The lower pole is water, the upper pole metal;
It is just a matter of harmonious stabilization of yin and yang.
If you succeed in combining firmness and flexibility,
In the center appears the heart of nirvana.

32. *Clear and Cloudy*

Clear water is celestial, cloudy water mundane;
How many students make a close investigation?
Where the pivotal works moves, real and false are divided;
Getting rid of the cloudy and keeping the clear produces white gold.

33. *Self-Refinement*

Practicing self-refinement is the first priority;
Stopping craving, forgetting emotions, removing entanglements,
When all attachment to the senses is cut off,
There is a single field of elixir, completely clean and clear.

34. *Setting Up the Foundation*

Stability of will is setting up the foundation;
Not wavering in body or mind is most excellent.
Rely on that in trouble and trial;
With no waves on still waters, there is no connection to things.

35. *Lead and Mercury*

True mercury is not mercury of the mundane world;
True lead is not lead that comes from mines.
One is sense, one essence, the primordial medicines;
Refining them, returning to the root, there is a great restoration.

36. *The Boy and Girl*

When the girl hides in FIRE, she is not real;
When the boy is in WATER, he cannot be followed.
But now that the opening of yin and yang has been explained,
By openness and solidity they give birth to the spiritual body.

37. *Water* ☵ *and Fire* ☲

Do not seek WATER and FIRE in the north and south.
The nature of fire is to fly up; water flows down.
If you can invert the two things,
Water rises, fire descends, and they form the elixir.

38. *Thunder* ☰☰ *and Lake* ☰☰

LAKE is not in the west, THUNDER not in the east;
When essence is disturbed and sense confused, their energies do
　　not join.
When you attain the method of restoring sense to essence,
In a moment you see the true inner self.

39. *Midnight and Noon*

Stop looking for midnight and noon in the night and day;
There is another indicator within the body.
There is yin and yang, movement and stillness, according to
　　the time;
In the midst of concentration you always hear the note of high
　　antiquity.

40. *Six A.M. and Six P.M.*

The classics say that bathing is done at six in the morning and
　　evening;
This describes two energies without the flaw of imbalance.
The ignorant who do not understand the meeting of yin and yang
Practice quiet sitting in the morning and at night.

41. *The Yellow Woman*

The pairing of female and male requires the yellow woman;
The central mediator forms the receptacle of creation.
If you ask for genuine information on the yellow woman,
Sincerity alone has the effect of harmonizing the five elements.

42. *Restoring the Elixir*

Why is cultivating the elixir called restoring the elixir?
When the five energies are separated, each is isolated;
When you know how to restore the original state, they all
　　combine—
Mind and body unwavering, they form into a whole.

43. *Maturation of the Elixir*

When the elixir has been restored, there is another method;
It does not require adjustment and further increase of yang.
The spiritual fire spontaneously burns in the furnace,
Sending forth a bead of light which suffuses the heavens.

44. *The Spiritual Embryo*

The spiritual embryo is not a corpuscle with form;
When energy clusters and spirit congeals, the true seed is
    planted.
Aware of perils, warding off danger, constantly taking care,
If you are too intent, it will surely cause disaster.

45. *Release from the Womb*

When the spiritual embryo is released and transmuted, then it is
    completely real;
Ten months of work nurtures the valley spirit.
Celestial energy totally pure, the force of mundanity exhausted,
An immortal being leaps out in open space.

46. *Doing*

Doing is not manipulation of the physical body;
Forced gymnastics all result in injury.
How can you understand the true secret, mentally transmitted?
Unfathomed by ghosts or spirits, one revolves yin and yang.

47. *Nondoing*

Nondoing is not sticking to indifferent emptiness;
When you are able to avoid negligence and obsession both,
Rooting out the seeds of repeated birth and death,
Right in the center there is just one spiritual youth.

48. *Return* ☷ *and Meeting* ☰

When yin culminates, returning to yang, advance the fire;
When yang is pure, on the verge of meeting, work the yin
    convergence.

When yin convergence and yang fire are used without error,
They forge the picture of the primordial absolute.

49. *Gentle and Vigorous*

Conquering demons by intense effort is vigorous cultivation;
Nurturing energy with empty mind is gentle development.
Knowing what is indicated and what is not, adapting to the
time,
Everywhere gold shines, the eyes are clear.

50. *Harmonizing Illumination*

Harmonizing illumination, merging with the ordinary world, is
the secret celestial mechanism;
The spiritual achievement of the great function is truly rare.
Ever responsive, ever clear, ever independent,
According to the time one sheds the old and dons new clothing.

ON THE TRUE OPENING OF THE MYSTERIOUS FEMALE

If students want to practice the great Tao and comprehend essence
and life, first they should find the opening of the mysterious
female. The opening of the mysterious female is the opening of the
mysterious pass.

This opening has a double door, opening and closing. It is nine
feet high and five feet wide. Outside is a spiritual officer on sentry;
inside are a dragon and tiger standing guard. The central hall is one
room which extends in all directions; in it dwells a true human,
with unkempt hair and bare feet, wearing a patchwork garment of
five colors and a belt of yellow silk, holding a scepter of golden
light, sitting peacefully on the chair of spontaneity, leaning back
without casting a shadow on the wall, a crystal lamp hung in front,
eyes half closed, immobile, at rest, not impulsively looking
around, not speaking at random. To the right there is a golden boy,
to the left a jade girl.

Sometimes the true human opens its eyes and light fills the universe, illumining even the dark regions of the netherworld. Sometimes the true human opens its mouth and energy fills the universe, putting all demons to flight. The true human holds the power of evolution, the mechanism of yin and yang, the talisman of life and death, the handle of essence and life.

However, there are few people in the world who are in genuine earnest. Most cannot put forth intensive effort or endure long perseverance; also they do not seek out the fundamental true principles, but just think of the mysterious pass and mysterious female in terms of physical locations and do some minor techniques which are attached either to voidness or to form, falsely imagining that they will attain the Tao thereby. This is pitiful.

If one is a true stalwart, one can decisively set aside all entanglements, so that all objects are empty, and concentrate on the matter of most urgent importance, call on true teachers, form associations with worthy companions, never changing one's determination; then one can eventually come to know the mysterious pass, see the mysterious female, and finally comprehend essence and life. Students should work on this.

ESSENTIAL TEACHINGS FOR CULTIVATING REALITY

The great Tao is uncontrived, based on spontaneity;
But until the work is complete, one cannot adapt with autonomy.
At the fork in the road, look for the true seed;
In the furnace of the eight trigrams, refine the heaven of essence.
The bottomless boat of method can cross the sea;
The medicines that come with the body can extend life.
Within punishment is hidden reward, which people can hardly
    fathom;
In harm arises blessing, which requires concentration.
The four forms blend, returning to the original state;

The five elements aggregate, growing a golden lotus.
Only when there is increase and decrease is it marvelous;
Only knowing what is indicated and what not can you enter the
mystery.
Shedding all defiling things which bind and envelop,
You attain the state of completeness before birth.
Cultivating immortality, becoming enlightened, all depends
on this;
Anything else is in vain, running to extremes.